How to Identify
Birds

Nicholas Hammond

Illustrated by
Michael Webb

Collins

HarperCollins Publishers Ltd
77-85 Fulham Palace Road
London W6 8JB

www.collins.co.uk

Collins is a registered trademark of
HarperCollins Publishers Ltd

6 5 4 3 2 1
11 10 09 08 07 06

A catalogue record for this book is available from the
British Library.

ISBN 0 00 719448 x

Editor: Emily Pitcher
Layout: Susie Bell
Proofreader: Katie Hardwicke
Index: Lisa Footitt

Reproduction by Colourscan, Singapore
Printed and bound by Printing Express, Hong Kong

Collins

Contents

How to use this book

The aim of this book is to enable people who know nothing about birds to be able to recognise 125 species that are relatively easy to see. Most of these are relatively common, but there are some that have been included because they are charismatic and well worth making an effort to see.

Keeping it simple is the basis on which this book is arranged. Identifying the species to which a bird belongs is not always easy. With some groups it becomes more difficult because there are several similar species. For beginners this can be overwhelming to the point of putting them off completely. The best way to learn about birds is to be shown them by an expert, but this is not always possible and being with an expert can be discouraging because they appear to find it all so simple.

The idea of this book is for the reader to become familiar with 33 key common species. Once you have learned these they will provide points of comparison with the 92 other species. For example, if you learn how to recognise a Starling, you will then be able to use it as a reference against which to identify the male Blackbird, female Blackbird, adult Song Thrush and juvenile Song Thrush.

Blackbird male (♂)

Starling

Adult Song Thrush

Blackbird female (♀)

Juvenile Song Thrush

The key species have been given two pages and the other species have a page each with look-alikes. This means that, having sorted the difference between Starling and Song Thrush, you will encounter the Song Thrush look-alikes – Mistle Thrush, Redwing and Fieldfare.

The process of identification is one of deduction and reduction. If you see a bird that you do not recognise as one of the 33 'key' species, the possible list is at least reduced by 33. But you may find that the unknown bird shares certain characteristics with one or more of the birds you already know.

Things to look for

Because many birds are colourful it is tempting to think that colour is the most important feature in identifying birds. The problem is that the light may vary from brilliant to dull to the point of darkness, and views may be fleeting. Size, shape, sound and the way the birds behave may be surer ways of identifying them.

Size – it may be very easy to judge the size of birds in the garden at the birdtable, but the further away the bird is the less easy it is to estimate its size. Thus in fields, on mudflats or out in the middle of a flooded gravel pit, size means very little unless there is more than one species present.

Although the measurements of each bird's length from bill-tip to tail-tip are given, judging size in the field can be very difficult. We have included a comparison in each description to the nearest key species in terms of size. The female mallard shown here is a key species against which other ducks (a female Shoveler and a female Teal) can be compared: all have speckled brown plumage, but there are clear differences in size as well as differences in shape.

Mallard *Shoveler* *Teal*

Shape – this is the first characteristic to look at because it helps to establish the family to which the bird belongs. There are several questions to ask about the shape of a bird. All birds have the same basic shape, but the proportions vary. There are small, compact species and there are large, slender species and a huge variety in between.

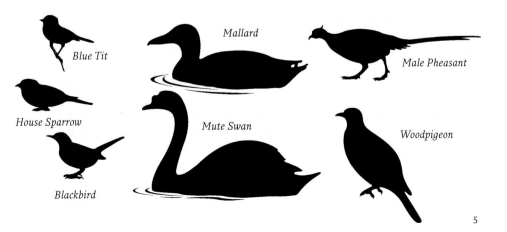

Blue Tit

Mallard

Male Pheasant

House Sparrow

Mute Swan

Woodpigeon

Blackbird

Bills – you will see from the illustration on p. 5 that even though each of these ducks has a flat bill the Shoveler's is much larger. This is because it feeds by sweeping the surface of the water to catch seeds and small aquatic animals. But as well as being a clue to the bird's eating habits bill shape is a good diagnostic feature.

Birds of prey and owls have hooked beaks for tearing flesh

Fish-eaters have bills that are long, strong and pointed or long and slightly hooked

Warblers, wagtails and other insect-eating birds have fine bills for snatching their prey

Finches have thick bills to crush the husks of seeds

The way birds behave – different species behave in different ways, which helps us to identify them. We need to look at the way they feed. For example, a bird with pointed wings hovering about 10 m above a roadside verge in Britain will be a Kestrel, while a bird of similar size soaring on rounded wings will be a Sparrowhawk. Both birds are hunting prey: the Kestrel is looking for small mammals to drop on to, while the Sparrowhawk is waiting for a small bird to swoop on. Both will also hunt from perches, with the Kestrel on a post or tree branch about to drop on an unsuspecting mouse, and the Sparrowhawk perched inconspicuously among branches in a hedgerow waiting to ambush a small bird.

The way birds fly is a particularly good clue. Woodpeckers, for example, have an undulating flight that is most obvious when they fly across an open space. By contrast, the Kingfisher flies fast and low over the water in a flight that is straighter than an arrow. Some species, such as starlings and waders, fly in tight flocks, wheeling in unison, while others such as finches fly in more ragged flocks.

Voice (and other noises) – songbirds sing to proclaim their possession of a territory and, in the early part of the breeding season, their need of a mate. Bird song is a sound of the spring and early summer, but a few species like the Robin sing throughout the year. Learning to recognise bird song is a good way to identify a species that you cannot see.

Most species make calls to contact other individuals or to warn them of danger. Bird calls are as important as song as a means to identification. Trying to put bird songs and calls into words is very difficult, but we have tried to describe the noises that birds make. It really is worth persevering with trying to learn songs and calls. There are recommendations for tapes and CDs at the end of the book.

Some birds use mechanical sounds to proclaim their presence. Snipe have stiffened tail feathers with which they can produce a drumming sound by diving from a height towards the ground. Others, such as Pheasants and Wood Pigeons, make whirring wing noises as they take off when they are flushed.

Where to see birds

Often the habitat in which you see the bird is a clue to its identity. While gannets are usually seen over the sea, freak happenings will displace birds and after a storm, for example, seabirds may be seen many miles inland. We have included some spreads where we show how birds use the habitats in which they can usually be found. These will give you another opportunity to compare similar species and learn about their behaviour.

Notes on species entries

Introductory paragraph – each entry has an introductory description of the bird and some points of interest about its life or history.

Where to see – this describes the species' favoured habitats and its distribution in the UK and Europe.

Voice – includes the song and the calls. There is an attempt to convey the sound it makes, either descriptively or phonetically.

Distribution maps – these offer a guide to where each bird can be found at different times of the year. *Green* indicates that the bird is resident and can be found all year round. *Orange* indicates that the bird is present only in the breeding season and migrates away in winter and back in spring. *Blue* indicates were the bird spends its time outside of the migration season, and *yellow* idicates where the bird is ony transient, passing through on its migration journey.

Illustrations – we have included as many illustrations as we can to show how the bird looks in different plumages and how it behaves. These have descriptive captions.

Fact File – *Scientific name* is important in that it describes the genus to which the bird belongs and the species. Thus the Blackbird is *Turdus merula* and the Song Thrush *Turdus philomelos* which shows that they are members of the same genus. *Family* shows which species belong to the same family. Blackbird and Song Thrush are both members of the thrush family, but so too is the Robin, although it is not in the same genus. *Length* and *wingspan* can be difficult to assess and are deceptive as diagnostic characteristics, but are given here as ways of making comparisons with similar-looking birds. *Nests* are included as matters of interest and not as an aid to identifying the birds. *Eggs* are described rather sketchily and are included as a matter of interest. More than one *Brood* of eggs may be laid in a season. *Food* can be an aid to identification, if you can see what the bird is actually eating.

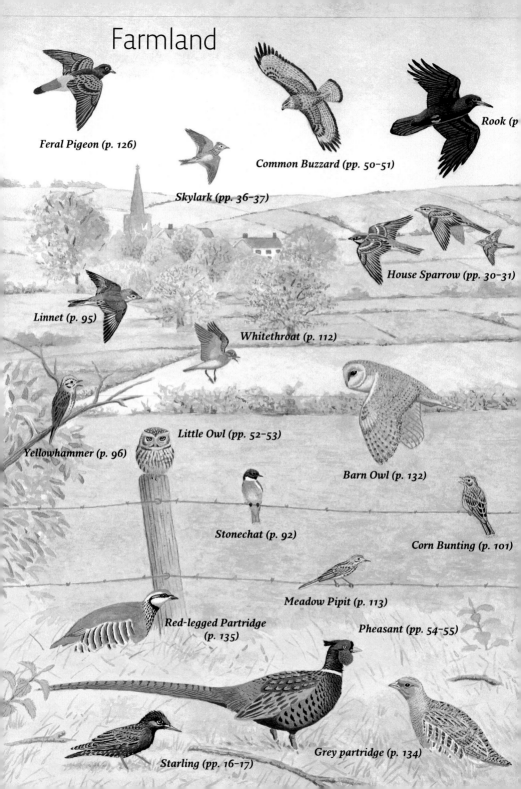

Farmland

Feral Pigeon (p. 126)

Common Buzzard (pp. 50-51)

Rook (p

Skylark (pp. 36-37)

House Sparrow (pp. 30-31)

Linnet (p. 95)

Whitethroat (p. 112)

Yellowhammer (p. 96)

Little Owl (pp. 52-53)

Barn Owl (p. 132)

Stonechat (p. 92)

Corn Bunting (p. 101)

Meadow Pipit (p. 113)

Red-legged Partridge
(p. 135)

Pheasant (pp. 54-55)

Starling (pp. 16-17)

Grey partridge (p. 134)

Red Kite (p. 130)

Woodpigeon (pp. 46-47)

Collared Dove (p. 124)

Turtle Dove (p. 125)

Kestrel (pp. 48-49)

Stock Dove (p. 127)

Mistle Thrush (p. 85)

Swallow (pp. 44-45)

Redwing (Winter only)
(p. 86)

atear (p. 93)

Pied Wagtail (pp. 38-39)

Fieldfare (Winter only)
(p. 87)

Greenfinch (pp. 28-29)

Goldfinch (p. 97)

Bullfinch (p. 94)

Chaffinch (pp. 26-27)

Woodland

Sparrowhawk (p. 131)

Carrion Crow (pp. 20–21)

Lesser Spotted
Woodpecker (p. 120)

Song Thrush (pp. 22–2)

Spotted Flycatcher (p. 89)

Blackbird (pp. 18–19)

Long-tailed Tit (p. 105)

Magpie (pp. 40–41)

Goldcrest (p. 107)

Redstart (p. 90)

Robin (pp. 24-25)

Wren (pp. 34–35)

Jay (p. 84)

Woodcock (p. 139)

Jackdaw (p. 82)

Tawny Owl (p. 133)

Green Woodpecker (p. 121)

Blue Tit (pp. 32-33)

Great Tit (p. 104)

Nuthatch (p. 122)

Treecreeper (p. 123)

Pied Flycatcher (p. 91)

Great Spotted
Woodpecker (pp. 42-43)

Chiffchaff (p. 111)

Blackcap (p. 109)

low Warbler (p. 110)

Garden Warbler (p. 108)

Dunnock (p. 88)

Estuary

Shelduck (p. 163)

Oystercatcher (p. 146)

Sanderling (p. 143)

Greylag Goose (p. 171)

Mute Swan (pp. 80–81)

Common Tern (p. 66–67)

Redshank (p. 140)

Ringed Plover
(summer plumage) (p. 148)

Grey Plover (p. 137)

Avocet (p. 147)

Little Ringed Plover
(summer plumage) (p. 149)

Bar-tailed Godwit (p. 141)

Wigeon (p. 165)

Turnstone (p. 144)

Lapwing (pp. 60–61)

Brent Goose (p. 170)

Dunlin (pp. 59–59)

Dunlin (pp. 58–59)

Canada Goose (pp. 78–79)

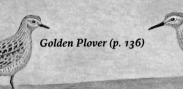

Common Sandpiper (p. 145)

Curlew (pp. 56–57)

Knot (p. 142)

Golden Plover (p. 136)

Shoveler (p. 162)

Snipe (p. 138)

Mallard (pp. 70–71)

Teal (p. 164)

Cliffs

Gannet (p. 169)

Puffins (p. 150)

Guillemot (pp. 62–63)

Common Gull (p. 154)

Fulmar (p. 152)

Guillemot (pp. 62–63)

Kittiwakes (p. 153)

Razorbill (p. 151)

Shag (p. 168)

Herring Gull (p. 155)

Cormorant (pp. 76–77)

Razorbill (p. 151)

Great Black-backed Gull (p. 157)

Lesser Black-backed Gull (p. 156)

Freshwater

Hobby (p. 129)

House Martin (p. 118)

Swift (p. 117)

Sand Martin (p. 119)

Reed Bunting (p. 100)

Kingfisher (p. 116)

Cuckoo (p. 128)

Grey Heron (pp. 74–75)

Reed Warbler (p. 103)

Great Crested Grebe (pp. 72–73)

Little Grebe (p. 161)

Sedge Warbler (p. 102)

Pochard (p. 167)

Coot (p. 160)

Moorhen (pp. 68–69)

Tufted Duck (p. 166)

Grey Wagtail (p. 114)

Yellow Wagtail (p. 115)

Starling

In spring adult ♂ have fewer speckles than ♀. Breast feathers are shaggy in spring

FACT FILE

Scientific name
Sturnus vulgaris

Family Starlings
(Sturnidae)

Length 20.5–22.5 cm

Nest In holes in trees,
buildings and
nestboxes

Eggs 5–7, pale blue

Broods 1–2 per year

Food Insects and
other invertebrates,
seeds and fruit

Voice Song is
chirping, whistling and
clicking. Often mimics
calls of other species.
Sings from prominent
perch, often with
wings held open

Where to see Towns,
gardens, woods and
farmland. Present
throughout the year,
but joined from
October to April by
flocks of migrants
from Europe. Roost in
flocks on buildings,
trees and reedbeds.
Flies in close flocks.

Mobs of chattering Starlings are a less common sight at the bird table than they once were, but they are still a characteristic bird of many gardens. The adult's black glossy plumage is speckled, the rather long, pointed bill is yellow and the legs are pink. In winter starlings are less glossy and more speckled. The juvenile is a plain grey-brown until the adult plumage begins to appear in the late summer giving a motley plumage.

Its stance is rather upright, its tail is short and its gait is bustling. The bill is used to probe the soil for insects and turn over leaves.

Grey-brown juvenile begging insistently for food. (As they moult into adult plumage the juveniles have a strangely motley appearance)

Winter plumage is more speckled and less glossy. Note the duller bill

LOOK-ALIKES

Blackbird ♂ (pp. 18-19) Chunkier. Browner. Less speckled.

Blackbird ♀ (pp. 18-19) Chunkier. Browner. Less speckled.

Song Thrush (pp. 22-23) Longer tail. Dark speckles on pale breast.

From late summer starlings form close, wheeling flocks

Song Thrush juvenile (p. 22) Speckles on back.

Short tail and short, pointed wings give an arrowhead impression in flight

Blackbird

Adult ♂ has black plumage, yellow bill, yellow eye-ring, longish tail. Larger than Starling

FACT FILE

Scientific name
Turdus merula
Family Thrushes and Chats (Turdidae)
Length 24–25 cm
Nest Cup-shaped, moss foundation and lined with mud and then grasses. Found between trunk and branch or on ledge of building
Eggs 3–5, blue usually mottled with red but may be variable
Broods 2–3 per year
Food Worms, insects and other invertebrates, berries, seeds and fruit
Voice Excellent singer with flute-like voice full of variety and varying between males. Sings from January to July; also produces a soft sub-song at other times
Where to see Gardens, woodlands, farmland, heath and moors across Europe, but rarely seen more than 200 metres from trees or bushes. Resident in western Europe, but eastern European and Scandinavian move south-west in winter.

One of the commonest, noisiest and most widespread of European birds, it must be one of the best known. Jet black males with yellow bills are relatively easy to identify. Females and young, being brown and having somewhat speckled plumage are easy to confuse with other species. The male's rich song makes it the best garden singer.

Juvenile has speckled breast but with darker background than Song Thrush. More ginger than ♀

Its tameness makes the Blackbird a favourite at the bird table and the relative frequency of albino and partially albino blackbirds mean that individuals can be identified. Blackbirds found in woodland are shyer than those in gardens, which will mob cats that threaten their young.

The Blackbird gives very noisy cries of alarm when disturbed. A soft whistle that is very hard to locate warns of the presence of birds of prey, while a repeated scolding note is often heard as it goes to roost in the evening.

Adult ♀ has brown plumage with pale throat and faint speckling bigger and more solid-looking than Song Thrush

LOOK-ALIKES

In sunny weather Blackbirds will sunbathe by spreading their wings out on the ground

Flight is rather jerky with wings rarely lifted higher than its back. Wings rather broad with squarer tips than other thrushes. Holds head noticeably high in flight. Always flicks up tail on landing

Adult **Starling (pp. 16-17)** Perky, upright stance with shorter tail and thinner bill.

Young **Starling (p. 16)** Paler than young Blackbird. Usually seen with adult.

Males will display vigorously in territorial disputes

Song Thrush (pp. 22-23) Speckles darker on paler background than ♀ Blackbird.

Dashes across a lawn, pauses to feed and moves on. Outside breeding season may be seen in open fields and parks, feeding in small flocks (rarely more than 15). Rootles among dead leaves for worms, insects and other small animals. It is often very noisy. Will feed on windfalls in very cold weather

Jackdaw (p. 82) Larger than Blackbird. Grey nape. Pale blue eyes. Black bill.

Carrion Crow

Adult is completely matt black

The Carrion Crow is one of only two completely black British birds (the other is the larger Raven). However, there is a grey and black race known as the Hooded Crow, which is found over much of Europe, including Ireland and the north of Scotland. Where their ranges overlap, the races interbreed producing various combinations of grey and black.

Carrion Crows are usually seen singly or in pairs. They are most likely to be seen in pairs at feeding places such as waste tips, where they are often seen with other members of the crow family.

Like all members of the crow family, the Carrion Crow has a very high learning ability.

Adult Hooded Crow has black head, wings and tail, and grey back, breast and underside

Gently rounded tail

Slow, laboured flight with a wing action like shallow rowing, calling with a hoarse 'kraa-kraa'

Hooded Crow

Carrion Crow

Nests high in trees are particularly noticeable in autumn and winter when the trees are bare. Old nests are often used by birds of prey, such as Kestrels

LOOK-ALIKES

Rook (p. 83) Pale, sharper bill. High forehead. Shaggy 'breeches'. Purple hue to plumage. More usually seen in flocks.

Jackdaw (p. 82) Noticeably smaller. Grey nape but less grey than Hoodie. Often seen in flocks.

These species may often be seen with Carrion Crows at feeding places and there is plenty of opportunity to compare them.

Black plumage has bluish gloss when fresh

Hops or walks on ground

Song Thrush

Adult has brown back with buff tips to wing coverts, buff breast with dark speckles, plain brown tail

FACT FILE

Scientific name
Turdus philomelos

Family Thrushes and Chats (Turdidae)

Length 20–22 cm

Nest Neat cup-shape of twigs, grasses and moss lined with mud, often built on a branch against the trunk

Eggs 3–5, pale, lightly spotted or speckled

Broods 2–3 per year

Food Worms, insects, snails, fruit, berries

Voice Call with a fine 'zit', less harsh than the Robin (see p. 24). Loud song with squeaky and shrill notes, few brief pauses and repeating phrases up to four times

Where to see This is a woodland bird that has adapted to live in gardens and farmland where there are trees and shrubs. The presence of snails and earthworms is important. Most Song Thrushes in western Europe are resident but those from northern and eastern Europe move southwards in winter.

This neat thrush has a creamy-white breast speckled with very dark brown spots, giving a vague impression of stripes down its body. Song Thrushes from mainland Europe are greyer than British ones.

A very able singer, the Song Thrush habitually repeats each song phrase three or four times. Its loud song is especially noticeable at dusk and some individuals will sing by the light of street lamps.

Outside the breeding season Song Thrushes may be seen feeding on earthworms on sports fields. These feeding flocks are never large and each bird keeps its distance from the others.

Fledgling has brown back with pale speckles

In flight, wings and back appear uniformly brown. Flight is direct with slight undulations. The patch in the 'armpit' beneath the wing appears to be pale orange or buff

Sings from a high perch. Often holds wings very slightly away from its body as it sings

Hops and runs on the ground. When feeding it runs, pauses, peers, probes the ground and moves on. Its stance is often upright

In summer, the Song Thrush holds the shells by the lip and smashes them against a hard surface

LOOK-ALIKES

Mistle Thrush (p. 85) Larger. Blotchier speckling. White outer tail feathers. Buff edges to flight feathers.

Redwing (p. 86) Rufous flanks and underwing. Noticeable pale eyebrow.

Blackbird ♀ (pp. 18-19) Larger. Darker. With fainter speckles. Always flicks tail when landing.

Fieldfare (p. 87) Larger. Grey head and rump. Fierce expression.

Robin

FACT FILE

Scientific name
Eritnacus rubecula
Family Thrushes and
chats (Turdidae)
Length 12.5-14 cm
Nest Cup of dead
leaves, mosses and
grasses in tree stump,
or variety of man-
made sites
Eggs 4-6, whitish,
with variable red
markings
Broods 2 per year
Food Invertebrates,
some seeds and fruit.
Likes cheese and
mealworms
Voice Melodious and
soft song. Short
repeated 'tic-tic-tic'
call
Where to see
Woodland species that
has become linked
with gardens in Britain
and Ireland, where it is
resident, being joined
in autumn by northern
and eastern European
migrants.

The red breast, perky posture and plump body make the Robin almost unmistakable. Its confiding nature and appearance on Christmas cards have made it the most familiar garden bird. The grubs, beetles and worms turned over by the gardener's fork encourage the Robin to approach close to people in search of food. Robins in mainland Europe tend to be more shy.

Males and females look alike, but when the birds are establishing territories and seeking mates they indulge in energetic, aggressive displays that help them to sort males from females. Both sexes sing and the Robin's melodious song can be heard throughout the year.

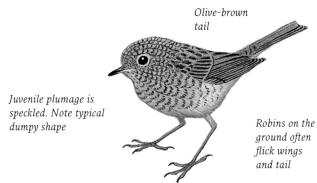

Olive-brown tail

Juvenile plumage is speckled. Note typical dumpy shape

Robins on the ground often flick wings and tail

In cold weather with its feathers plumped (far left), the Robin looks plump, but it can be quite slim at other times of year (left)

Very determined in defence of its territory, the Robin chooses prominent perches with good views of its territory from which to sing

Aggression between individuals focuses on red breasts, which each bird tries to exaggerate

Seen from behind the Robin has a dumpy appearance

LOOK-ALIKES

Dunnock (p. 88)
Grey breast and face. Streaked back and flanks. Less bold and stance less upright.

Wren (pp. 34–35)
Much smaller. Dumpier with short tail.

Redstart (p. 90)
Buffish breast. Red tail. Usually in woodland or woodland edges.

Chaffinch

Adult ♂ has pink breast, grey-blue head and white wing-bars, white outer tail feathers and an olive rump in both sexes. Bill becomes grey-blue in breeding plumage

FACT FILE

Scientific name
Fringilla coelebs

Family Finches
(Fringillidae)

Length 15 cm

Nest Neat cup of grasses and roots decorated with lichens, usually in the crook of a branch

Eggs 4–5, bluish, and streaked with purplish-brown

Broods 1–2 per year

Food Seeds, fruit and small insects

Voice Ringing, far-carrying song with flourishes in local 'dialect' repeated regularly. Call from a perch is a high-pitched 'pink', and a fairly unobtrusive 'jupp' in flight.

Where to see One of the most abundant and widespread of British breeding birds, the Chaffinch is found in woods, farmland, open country with bushes and gardens. British breeders rarely move far from where they were bred, but Scandinavian and eastern European birds move south-westwards in autumn, usually in flocks in which all birds are the same sex.

Adult ♀ has a pale breast and an olive rump

In breeding plumage the male Chaffinch is striking. The female has a subtler plumage of olive and browns, but she also has double wing–bars and white outer tail feathers. Chaffinches can be trusting and will often cadge scraps in town parks, picnic sites and car parks.

In autumn, males look faded, but over the winter they become brighter and the feathers become worn, giving way to brighter colours. In winter, they are often seen in flocks.

White wing-bars and outer tail feathers are obvious in both sexes in flight (right)

Chaffinches have a distinctive rising and falling flight, with the wings being closed between flaps

Song is delivered throughout the breeding season

Chaffinches feed in flocks with other finches outside the breeding season, in farmland or on the edge of woodlands

Rather hunched posture when feeding on the ground, moving in jerky hops

LOOK-ALIKES

Bullfinch ♂ (p. 94) Bright pink breast. Black cap. White rump. Chunky build.

Bullfinch ♀ (p. 94) Brown breast. Black cap. White rump. Chunky build.

Linnet (p. 95) Red breast. Red forehead. Brown neck.

Greenfinch juvenile **(pp. 28-29)** Streaked breast. Thicker bill. Yellow wing flash.
Pied Flycatcher ♀ (p. 91) Big eyes. Black bill. More compact shape. Finer bill.

Greenfinch

Adult ♀ has a thick bill, faint streaks on breast and a green rump

Adult ♂ (left) has a thick bill, green head and back and a yellowish green breast

Its powerful, husk-cracking bill and thick-set neck give the Greenfinch an almost stocky appearance. The legs and tail are comparatively short, and it can look almost clumsy on the ground, but can be acrobatic on bird feeders.

The breeding plumage of males is bright green with yellow wing flashes. Females are less brightly coloured while the streaked juvenile may be grey-brown and look rather sparrow-like. In winter, they are usually seen in flocks.

Juvenile has a streaked breast

♂ displays over treetops with slow wing-beats

In flight, which is bounding, it looks bulky and yellow flashes on wings and tail show well

Frequently visits bird tables, particularly enjoying sunflower seeds and peanuts

LOOK-ALIKES

Chaffinch ♀ (pp. 26-27) No obvious streaking. White wing flashes.

House Sparrow (pp. 30-31) Slighter. No yellow.

Siskin (p. 98) Smaller. Yellow wing bars. Black cap.

Goldfinch (p. 97) Neater yellow wing bars and black on wings in all plumages. Crimson face.

House Sparrow

♀ has pale eyebrow and no black

♂ in summer has a large black bib, a grey crown and a grey rump (country sparrows tend to be brighter than those in towns)

FACT FILE

Scientific name
Passer domesticus

Family Sparrows and Weaver Finches (Passeridae)

Length 14–16 cm

Nest Untidy dome nest in buildings and bushes

Eggs 3–5, greyish, with uniform marks

Broods 3 per year

Food Seeds, buds, fruit and insects

Voice Simple cheeping and chattering notes

Where to see
Wherever man lives in Europe you are likely to see the House Sparrow. It is a resident in the UK, but outside the breeding season flocks form and forage in farmland.

House Sparrows are Eurasian birds and are now found on all continents. They seem to have ample time to sit around thinking of ways of tackling new sources of food, such as flying insects or nuts in hanging feeders, which are usually taken by more agile species. However, numbers of House Sparrows in the UK fell at the end of the 20th century for reasons that are yet unclear.

♂ in winter has less extensive bib

Fine white wing-bar shows in flight

Males take part in noisy courtship of females

LOOK-ALIKES

Reed Bunting ♂ **(p. 100)** Black cap. Throat with white moustache. Looks more slender.

Reed Bunting ♀ **(p. 100)** Buff moustache. Longer tail. More slender build.

Chaffinch ♀ **(pp. 26–27)** Slighter. More olive. Finer bill.

Greenfinch juvenile **(pp. 28–29)** Greenish tinge. Yellow wing flashes.
Dunnock (p. 88) Grey breast. Rounder build. Finer bill.

Blue Tit

Adult has blue wings and blue cap and a yellow breast with smudgy black stripe

The commonest of the British tits, the Blue Tit is a familiar bird table visitor. In winter, Blue Tits that have bred in woodlands move into gardens to take advantage of food put out by people. More individuals than most of us realise pass through a garden: a study showed that over 1000 individual birds passed through one garden in a year, but usually no more than six were to be seen at one time.

Juvenile has a yellow face and a blue-green cap

In flight it has a faint white wing-bar, translucent blue wing and a green back

A parent feeds sawfly larva to a juvenile that has recently left the nest and is begging by cheeping and wing-quivering

LOOK-ALIKES

Great Tit (p. 104) Bigger. Brighter. Black-headed. Distinct band down breast.

Coal Tit (p. 105) Large head. Black cap. No blue.

Goldcrest (p. 107) Smaller. Olive green. Very fine bill.

Blue Tits are agile feeders, able to hang upside down to feed on insects at the tips of branches

Wren

Adult has a pale stripe above the eye, a barred back, a cocked tail and a slightly curved-down bill. Sexes look similar

FACT FILE

Scientific name
Troglodytes troglodytes
Family Wrens
(Troglodytidae)
Length 9–10 cm
Nest Dome of leaves, grasses and mosses in hollow or crevice
Eggs 5–8, white, speckled
Broods 2 per year
Food Insects, spiders
Voice Call is a repeated hard 'tic' or 'clink'. Song is a rapid, surprisingly loud series of metallic warbling notes
Where to see Wrens are found throughout most of Europe wherever there is suitable cover, but most favoured are damp deciduous or mixed woods, with dense undergrowth. Some populations are resident, others move south in winter.

The Wren is very small and feeds in vegetation, often close to the ground. In its short flights between feeding places the rapidly whirring wings give the impression of a very large bumblebee. Its cocked tail and tiny size makes confusion with other species fairly unlikely.

Male Wrens are most obvious when they are singing. The song is a loud, prolonged succession of high notes delivered from bushes, hedges and fences.

Searching on the ground for insects, at first glance the quick-moving Wren can sometimes look like a mouse

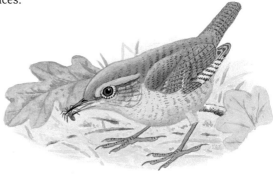

Whirring flight gives the Wren the appearance of a large bee

♂ singing from a bush, delivering noisy, cheerful song

Dome-shaped nest

Skylark

FACT FILE

Scientific name
Alauda arvensis

Family Larks
(Alaudidae)

Length 18-19 cm

Nest Shallow cup on
ground lined with
grass

Eggs 3-5, white, and
thickly spotted with
green

Broods 2-4 per year

Food Seeds, insects

Voice Chirruping call.
Warbling song in flight
from dawn to dusk,
from midwinter
through midsummer
into July

Where to see
Skylarks breed on
arable farmland,
pasture, golf courses,
airfields and inland
grassland. In autumn
flocks are formed and
the larks feed on
stubble and ploughed
fields. The birds that
breed in Eastern
Europe move south-
ward in winter. Earlier
cropping of cereals has
deprived Skylarks of
breeding areas.

The song of the Skylark above open country is a typical sound of
spring and summer. The sharp-eyed can focus on the singing bird
as he ascends, but he may rise high enough not to be seen. On the
ground the streaked plumage makes it very difficult to see and the
best views are often when it is seen at the roadside.

When there is thick snow the ground-feeding Skylark moves
southwards to snow-free areas. In very hard winters this may
mean moving to southern Europe. In Britain, right up until the
19th century, large numbers of winter flocks were trapped in nets
and used as food.

Loud, far-carrying song is delivered as the lark hovers, often high enough to be invisible to the human eye. Note how the wings look pointed. They also sing from posts

LOOK-ALIKES

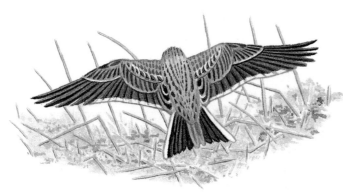

Corn Bunting (p. 101) Much chunkier. Dangles legs in flight.

In flight, white outer tail feathers and white trailing edge to wings can be seen from the rear

Meadow Pipit (p. 113) Smaller. No white trailing edge to wings.

Skylarks walk with purposeful stride, but will crouch mouse-like and shuffle forward when feeding in exposed places

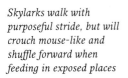

House Sparrow ♀ (pp. 30-31) More squat. Thick bill.

Pied Wagtail

FACT FILE

Scientific name
Motacilla alba

Family Wagtails and
Pipits (Motacillidae)

Length 18 cm

Nest Cup of twigs,
grass and leaves in
hole or crevice

Eggs 5-6

Broods 2 per year

Food Insects and
other invertebrates

Voice Call is a
double-noted
'chissick' or a triple-
noted 'chi-chi-ssick'.
Song is a simple
twittering phrase
followed by a pause
and then more twitters

Where to see Breeds
from coasts to upland
streams including sites
such as city centres
and gardens. They are
often seen near water.
Outside the breeding
season they spend the
day searching for food
individually or in pairs,
but they roost in flocks
in trees, glasshouses
and packing sheds.

*♂ in summer has
black chin and
throat and black
tail with white
outer tail feathers*

One of the most elegant of the birds to be seen in parks and
gardens, the male Pied Wagtail in breeding plumage is difficult to
confuse with other species. Females, especially in winter, and
juveniles may be confused with other wagtails. The harsh
'chissick' call is distinctive. In continental Europe, the male has a
slatey-grey back.

This wagtail's choice of nest-sites is wide - from holes and
crevices in natural sites to artificial sites such as ledges in
buildings and behind flowerpots in greenhouses. Pied
Wagtails catch insects by running after them
and picking them up, and from plants
growing close to the ground.

*♀ in summer has
dark grey back*

In winter, Pied Wagtails spend the days foraging in small groups, returning at night to large communal roosts in warm, well-lit places

First-winter Pied Wagtail has a rudimentary dark throat-patch

Distinctive walk in which tail wags and head jerks mechanically backwards and forwards

Juvenile has greyish plumage and white eyebrow

LOOK-ALIKES

Grey Wagtail ♂ **(p. 114)** Yellow rump. Single wing-bar. Slimmer build. Yellow breast.

Yellow Wagtail ♂ **(p. 115)** Eyebrow. Pale yellow breast.

Magpie

Adult has glossy, greenish blue-black plumage, white belly and white patches on wings

FACT FILE

Scientific name
Pica pica

Family Crows (Corvidae)

Length 40–50 cm (inc. 20–30 cm tail)

Nest Large dome of sticks lined with mud, grasses and plants, in bushes and trees

Eggs 5–7, pale blue blotched with olive

Broods 1 per year

Food Seeds, fruit, insects, carrion, eggs, nestlings

Voice Call is a fast staccato series of very hoarse notes

Where to see
Magpies are widely spread across Europe in areas where there are trees and bushes. It is a common bird in England, Wales and Ireland, but is scarce in Scotland except in the central lowlands.

This handsome, noisy, black-and-white bird is difficult not to notice, even if some people find it difficult to love due to its habit of feeding on young songbirds. It is always wary, but is not timid, often venturing near houses. Magpies stealing silver and jewellery is a myth, but one which nonetheless demonstrates that they have a well-developed ability to learn.

Juvenile has shorter tail than adults

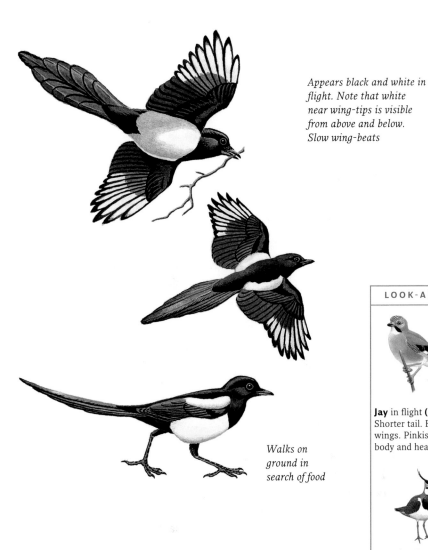

Appears black and white in flight. Note that white near wing-tips is visible from above and below. Slow wing-beats

Walks on ground in search of food

Perches in trees. Note the graduated tail feathers giving the long triangular shape

LOOK-ALIKES

Jay in flight **(p. 84)** Shorter tail. Blue on wings. Pinkish brown body and head.

Lapwing (pp. 60-61) No white on upperside of wings. Short tail.

Great Spotted Woodpecker (pp. 42-43) Smaller. Undulating flight. Different shape.

Great Spotted Woodpecker

FACT FILE

Scientific name
Dendrocops major

Family Woodpeckers
(Picidae)

Length 23–26 cm

Wingspan 38–44 cm

Nest In hole excavated
in tree-trunk

Eggs 4–7, white

Broods 1 per year

Food Insects, pine-
nuts, nestlings, bird-
table seeds and suet

Voice Call is a sharp,
single 'chek'. To
proclaim its territory
and attract a mate, it
uses its bill to drum
against a hollow trunk
in short bursts of
between 0.4 and 0.8
seconds

Where to see In
Britain the Great
Spotted Woodpecker is
most likely to be seen
in deciduous
woodland, but in the
remainder of Europe it
is found in all types of
woodland. Absent
from Scotland. It is a
resident and will visit
garden feeders in
winter.

*Adult ♀ displays no
red patch on its nape*

*Adult ♂ has a red
patch on its nape*

This is one of the most spectacularly patterned (and unmistakable)
birds to be seen in gardens. Its natural habitat is woodland of all
types. It has feet with two toes pointing forwards and two pointing
backwards which, with the stiffened tail feathers, allows it to hang
onto the trunks of trees and
move vertically upwards.
The bill is strong
enough to hack at
rotten wood and
reach grubs of
insects.

*Juvenile has a red cap
and less well-defined
plumage patterns*

The flight of the Great Spotted Woodpecker is undulating. This is particularly noticeable when flying in more open areas

The Great Spotted Woodpecker is agile, often feeding on the underside of branches and on hanging bird-feeders

LOOK-ALIKES

Jay (p. 84) Larger. Blue on wings. Pinkish brown.

Lesser Spotted Woodpecker (p. 120) Smaller (sparrow-sized). Barred wings.

Nuthatch (p. 122) Blue-grey. Orange. Smaller.

Green Woodpecker (p. 121) Larger. Green. Longer neck.

White patches are clearly seen on the back of a Great Spotted Woodpecker climbing up a tree trunk. Note the stiffened tail being used as a prop and the feet adapted for climbing tree trunks

Swallow

FACT FILE

Scientific name
Hirundo rustica

Family Swallows and
Martins (Hirundidae)

Length 17-21 cm (inc.
3-6 cm tail)

Nest Cup of tiny
pellets of mud lined
with feathers on
rafters in outbuildings

Eggs 4-5, with reddish
spots

Broods 2-3 per year

Food Insects

Voice Loud twittering
song and single-note
calls

Where to see
Swallows are found in
farmland areas where
there are plenty of
insects and buildings
in which to nest. They
are visitors to Britain
and Ireland between
late March and
October. In autumn,
Swallows gather on
telegraph wires and
reed beds before
migrating.

*Adult has very dark back and
wings, a deep red face with dark
blue collar and a long, finely
forked tail which is longer in ♂
than ♀ (top left)*

Swallows are summer visitors from southern Africa - an
extraordinary 5,000 mile journey, which they make twice a year.
They are swift, beautiful, streamlined birds that often fly close to
the ground or over water in search of flying insects that they catch
in their broad gapes.

Their long tail
streamers are unlike
any of the related
species.

*Young have
reddish buff faces
and shorter tails*

Swallow nests are made of pellets of mud and have an open top (unlike House Martins', see p. 118)

see p. 118

In flight, wings are pointed and tails are long

In autumn, Swallows and Martins gather on telegraph wires before migrating. Swallows have longer tails than House Martins

Wood Pigeon

The adult has a plumbeous breast, white marks on either side of neck with a blurred metallic green nape. The sexes look alike

FACT FILE

Scientific name
Columba palumbus

Family Pigeons and Doves (Columbidae)

Length 38-43 cm

Wingspan 68-77 cm

Nest Flimsy-looking raft of twigs in a tree

Eggs 2, white

Broods 3 per year

Food Seeds, grain, plant material

Voice Song is a five-syllable low cooing – 'coo-coo, coo-coo... cooo' repeated between 3 and 5 times. The alarm call is a mechanical sound made by clattering the wings loudly

Where to see Found across Europe except the far north, as a resident in the west and the Mediterranean, and as a summer visitor in eastern Europe and Scandinavia. Breeds in areas with trees, including farmland, woods, parks and gardens.

Larger than the domesticated town pigeon, the Wood Pigeon is a stocky, rather handsome pigeon with a large body that makes its head look small. It is found in both town and country. In flight it can be confused with other species, including birds of prey. It breeds throughout the year if the conditions are right, and large flocks of European breeders move south-west in winter to feed in farmland. The nest of the Wood Pigeon is a raft of twigs which looks rather flimsy.

Juvenile has no white mark on the neck

Flying flocks of Wood Pigeons are a common sight in farmland in winter

Feral Pigeon (p. 126) Double bar on wings. Many plumage variations.

In flight, white bars show across the wings, which have black tips. Note the broad black band on the tail

Stock Dove (p. 127) Smaller. No white neck marks.

Stock Dove in flight **(p. 127)** No white bars on wings. Dark trailing edge and wing-tips.

Displaying Wood Pigeon rises steeply, claps its wings loudly at the apex, and glides down

Collared Dove (p. 124) Smaller. Buffish-grey. Narrow black collar.

Turtle Dove (p. 125) Smaller. More slender. Black-and-white collar. Tortoiseshell back.

Kestrel

Scientific name
Falco tinnunculus

Family Falcons
(Flaconidae)

Length 31–37 cm

Wingspan 68–78 cm

Nest Bare ledge, hole
in tree, old crow's
nest, specially
constructed nestbox

Eggs 4–5, white,
heavily blotched with
brown

Broods 1 per year

Food Small mammals,
reptiles, birds and
large insects

Voice Sharp repeated
'kee-kee-kee-kee'

Where to see
Widespread across
Europe (except for the
far north of
Scandinavia and
Iceland) in open
country. Much of the
population is resident,
but northern and
eastern European
Kestrels move south
in winter.

*Adult ♂ has a grey head
with small black moustache,
a grey rump and tail, a
black band on end of tail,
black spots on a chestnut
back and yellow feet with
black claws*

Probably the most commonly seen bird of
prey in Europe, this small falcon is a bird of
open country, where it hunts its prey by
hovering head-to-wind and dropping to the
ground when it sees a movement in the grass. It
often nests on buildings and several English cathedrals can boast
nesting kestrels. The plumage differences make it fairly simple to
sex Kestrels in the field.

*Adult ♀ has a brown head with
a small black moustache, a
barred brown tail, a brown back
with dark speckles on back and
yellow feet with black claws*

In soaring flight the wings have rounded edges which can cause confusion with a Sparrowhawk

Hovers on pointed wings when hunting, facing into the wind, before dropping onto its prey

Will also hunt from a perch by dropping onto its prey

LOOK-ALIKES

Sparrowhawk in flight **(p. 131)** Rounded wings.

Hobby in flight **(p. 129)** Pointed wings look broader near body. Medium-sized. More square-cut tail.

Cuckoo in flight **(p. 128)** Broader tail. Crescent-shaped wings.

Common Buzzard (pp. 50-51) Much larger. More thickset. No contrast between breast and upperparts.

Common Buzzard

Breast is finely barred, bill is yellow tipped with black and feet are yellow with black claws

FACT FILE

Scientific name
Buteo buteo

Family Hawks
(Accipitridae)

Length 46–58 cm

Wingspan 110–132 cm

Nest Bulky cup of
sticks and twigs in tree
or on rocky ledge

Eggs 3–4, white
blotched with red

Broods 1 per year

Food Small mammals

Voice Loud mewing
call falling in pitch,
mainly in spring

Where to see
Widespread across
Europe except for
Iceland, much of
Ireland and
mountainous areas of
Scandinavia. Resident
in the west. Summer
visitor to much of
Scandinavia and
eastern Europe.

This large, round-winged, compact bird of prey is widespread
across Europe and is now spreading eastwards from upland areas
in England. On the continent, the plumage shows great variation
and Common Buzzards may vary from dark brown to cream, with
a variety of combinations.

Buzzards show great variation in colouration between pale and dark

In flight adults show narrow band on tail, dark patches under the wing and 'fingered' wings

Wings held in shallow 'V' in soaring flight

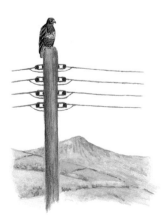

Often seen perched on posts or telegraph poles

LOOK-ALIKES

Sparrowhawk (p. 131) Smaller. Rounded unfingered wings.

Red Kite (p. 130) Longer. Slightly bent wings. Deep fork to tail.

Carrion Crow (pp. 20-21) Shallow wing-beats. Pointed bill.

Tawny Owl (p. 133) Rounded wings. Large head.

Little Owl

*Adult has noticeable pale
eyebrows, spots on wings
and smaller white spots
on head*

*It has an upright posture
and a crouching posture
that give it very different
shapes*

The smallest owl to be found in Britain was introduced to
Northamptonshire in the late 19th century from Europe, where it
is now widespread. No larger than a Blackbird, it is found in
farmland and woodland edges across England and Wales. It is
partially diurnal and its habit of perching in a prominent position –
such as on a post or telegraph post – mean that it may be the most
frequently seen owl in some parts. The Little Owl's diet varies
greatly and includes worms, larger insects, small rodents, frogs
and small birds.

In flight there is a pale narrow collar around the nape, and narrow light bars between the body and wings

Flight is bounding. Note broad wings

Adult brings food to young. Often seen in family parties in late summer

LOOK-ALIKES

Tawny Owl (p. 133)
Larger. Proportionately larger head.

Barn Owl (p. 132)
Larger. Heart-shaped face. Very pale.

Kestrel ♀ (pp. 48-49)
Long tail. Smaller head. Barred plumage.

Song Thrush (pp. 22-23) Speckled breast. Very differently shaped face.

Pheasant

'Ring-neck' ♂ has distinct white collar, green head and red wattle around the eye. Note tail is comparatively longer than females

♀ is mottled brown and has shorter tail

FACT FILE

Scientific name
Phasianus colchicus

Family Partridges and Pheasants (Phasianidae)

Length ♂ 66–90 cm (inc. tail at 35–45 cm), ♀ 55–70 cm (inc. tail at 20–25 cm)

Wingspan 70–90 cm

Nest Hollow in ground

Eggs 7–15, pale olive, with no markings

Broods 1 per year

Food Seeds, shoots, berries

Voice Hoarse two-syllable cry with emphasis on the last syllable

Where to see Pheasants are widespread across Britain except for the far north of Scotland, and are found across continental Europe from France to Eurasia, with isolated populations in Spain.

The male Pheasant is probably the most brightly coloured of the birds found in the British countryside, but it is not a native species. It was probably brought to Britain by the Normans and has since been extensively reared for shooting and is now widespread. The females are smaller and a well-camouflaged brown. The young (or poults) are capable of flying before they reach adult size. Plumages of the males vary considerably because there are several varieties of reared Pheasants.

Young Pheasants, or poults, have speckled plumage similar to ♀, but have no tail

Pheasants rise steeply, and noisily, from the ground when they are flushed. Note how tails of both ♂ and ♀ spread in flight

Several varieties of Pheasant have been released on shooting estates, some of which lack the 'ring neck'

The dark green variety looks almost black in some lights

LOOK-ALIKES

Grey Partridge in flight **(p. 134)** Short tail. Smaller.

Red-legged Partridge in flight **(p. 135)** Short tail. Smaller. Orange marks on tail.

Grey Partridge (p. 134) No tail. Smaller. Comparatively smaller head with orange face.

Red-legged Partridge in flight **(p. 135)** No tail. Smaller. Orange marks on tail. Comparatively smaller head with white face.

Curlew

Adult has noticeable down-curved bill (longer in ♂ than ♀), long legs and rather pale markings on face

FACT FILE

Scientific name
Numenius arquata

Family Sandpipers
and their allies
(Scolopacidae)

Length 48–57 cm
(inc. bill of 9–15 cm)

Wingspan 89–106 cm

Nest Hollow in
ground lined with
grasses

Eggs 4, olive,
blotched brown

Broods 1 per year

Food Worms,
molluscs, crabs

Voice The call is a
far-carrying, fluting
'cur-lii'

Where to see Breeds
in moorland, open
marshland and water
meadows in western
and northern Britain
and Ireland. When
moving south in
autumn and north
again in spring,
Curlews are seen on
coasts. Some birds
stay around the British
coasts throughout the
winter months.

The downward-curving bill of the Curlew is very distinctive. That of the female is longer than that of the male. The Curlew uses its bill to probe the mud in search of worms and other invertebrates. The difference in bill length between the sexes enables Curlews to exploit food at different depths. This is one of the larger wading birds seen in Britain.

When feeding it bends forward and the bill disappears into the mud

The call of the Curlew is distinctive

In flight it has extensive white rump and feet protruding beyond end of tail. Often flies in flocks in winter

Curlews feed on worms and molluscs in tidal flats in winter

When the tide covers their feeding grounds, they have nowhere to feed and roost in flocks on dry ground

LOOK-ALIKES

Bar-tailed Godwit in flight **(p. 141)** Slightly up-curved bill. Comparatively shorter legs.

Bar-tailed Godwit (p. 141) Slightly up-curved bill. Greater contrast between darkness of wing-tips and the remainder of the wings.

Snipe (p. 138) Long straight bill. Smaller. Often flies in zig-zag.

Redshank (p. 140) Shorter. Straight bill. Red legs. White patches on wings.

Dunlin

Adult in summer has a black belly, rufous chestnut back flecked with black and a slightly down-curved black bill

Adult in winter is drab, with its grey back and pale underside

FACT FILE

Scientific name
Calidris alpina

Family Sandpipers and their allies (Scolopacidae)

Length 17-21 cm

Wingspan 32-36 cm

Nest Hollow on ground

Eggs 4, greenish blotched with brown

Broods 1 per year

Food Molluscs, crustaceans

Voice Rasping 'chrreet'

Where to see Breeds in moorlands and tundra and moves southwards in autumn. Adults migrate in July and August and juveniles migrate from late August to October. Outside the breeding season it is found in a variety of coastal and marshy habitats.

The commonest small wader to be found around the British coastline, the Dunlin is usually seen in flocks around the coast outside the breeding season. It breeds in tundra and moorlands. In breeding plumage it is a striking bird with a dark breast and chestnut back, but it is duller during the rest of the year.

Juveniles have black spots on breast. The intensity of the spots varies between individuals

In flight there are narrow white bars on each wing and a black mark along the rump and tail

In flight summer adults show black bellies

LOOK-ALIKES

Knot (p. 142) Dumpy body. Shorter bill. More uniformly grey in winter.

Sanderling (p. 143) Pale grey and white. Black bill and legs.

Common Sandpiper (p. 145) Long body. Short legs. Longer tail which it flicks up and down.

Redshank (p. 140) Longer. Orange legs. Mottled breast.

Birds moulting between summer and winter plumage have a motley plumage

Lapwing

♀ in summer has slightly shorter crest and less well-defined throat markings

Adult ♂ in summer has a long crest, metallic green upperside amd a black throat and bib

FACT FILE

Scientific name
Vanellus vanellus

Family Plovers
(Charadriidae)

Length 28–31 cm

Wingspan 67–72 cm

Nest Depression in ground

Eggs 4, buff with dark blotches

Broods 1 per year

Food Worms, insects and other invertebrates

Voice Call is a sharp 'pee-wit' and song is a variation of this

Where to see Breeds on arable, pasture, moorland and coastal marshes across northern Europe. Forms large flocks in winter feeding in marshland and on farmland.

The 'pee-wit' call of the Lapwing was once a common sound of early spring in the pastures where it nests, but changing farming practices have made this beautiful bird less common in Britain. In winter, flocks of Lapwings in flight seem to shimmer as the birds wheel to show alternately the darkness of the upper sides of their wings, then the lightness of the underside. Once learned, the field characteristics of the Lapwing are unmistakable.

Adult in winter has a shorter crest, pale fringes to green feathers on back and a blurred throat and bib

Lapwings fly in tight flocks that wheel and twist, giving a flickering impression as the dark uppersides of the birds and pale underside alternate

Broad, rounded wings are a distinctive characteristic of flying Lapwings

Breeding pairs display over fields with tumbling flights

In winter, flocks gather on fields, sometimes in company with Golden Plovers and Black-headed Gulls

LOOK-ALIKES

Turnstone (p. 144) 'Tortoiseshell' back. Less upright stance. In coastal habitats.

Oystercatcher (p. 146) Distinctly black and white. Long orange bill.

Ringed Plover (p. 148) Smaller. No crest.

Golden Plover (p. 136) Slimmer. Golden tinge to back.

Guillemot

Adult in breeding plumage has a chocolate-brown head and upperparts and a white breast

Of all the birds in the northern hemisphere, the Guillemot is the most like a penguin. But unlike a penguin it has wings that are powerful enough for flight. Underwater, the Guillemot and other members of the auk family use their wings to swim in pursuit of small fish. Guillemots spend most of their lives at sea, returning to the cliffs of western and northern Britain to breed between February and early August.

In winter, adult loses brown on face and much of head, and flanks become more streaked

From below looks pale with slightly darker primaries

In flight from above, the Guillemot looks dark brown, shows white on either side of the rump and has white trailing edge to wing. Note narrow wings

LOOK-ALIKES

Puffin (p. 150) Smaller. Rounder with large bill. No white on wings.

Razorbill (p. 151) Blacker. Thicker bill.

Lesser Black-backed Gull (p. 156) White head. Broader wings. Different shape.

Guillemots nest in crowded colonies on cliff-ledges

Oystercatcher in flight (p. 146) Extensive white wing-bars. Long, orange-red bill.

Some individuals have narrow pale markings around the eyes. They are described as bridled

63

Black-headed Gull

Adult in winter has blotched marks on its head and a black tip to red bill

Adult in summer has chocolate-brown head, red legs and a red bill

FACT FILE

Scientific name
Larus ridibundus
Family Gulls (Laridae)
Length 35–39 cm
Wingspan 86–99 cm
Nest Cup of vegetation or scrape in ground
Eggs 3, cream, with dark blotches
Broods 1 per year
Food Invertebrates, seeds, rubbish
Voice Strident, angry-sounding 'keeahr'
Where to see Resident across much of the British Isles, breeding at inland sites such as shallow lakes and marshes. Migrants from northern and eastern Europe move south and west in winter.

Throughout most of the year this gull is found across Europe. It is seen both inland and along low-lying sea coasts and is the gull most frequently seen following the plough. It has a dark chocolate-brown head rather than black. In winter, all that remains of the head are two blurred vertical lines. Juveniles are predominantly blotched with brown and grey.

Juveniles have pale underparts, unlike many other immature gulls which have mottled underparts

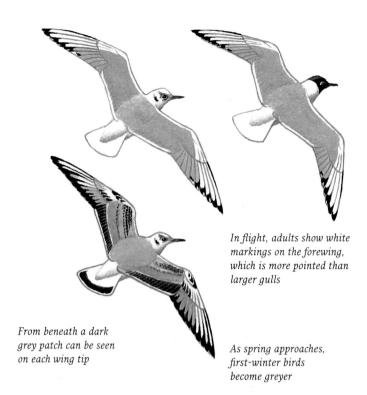

In flight, adults show white markings on the forewing, which is more pointed than larger gulls

From beneath a dark grey patch can be seen on each wing tip

As spring approaches, first-winter birds become greyer

Black-headed gulls nest in colonies and mating birds perform vigorous displays

LOOK-ALIKES

Herring Gull in winter (p. 155) Black and white marks on wing tips. White trailing edge. Larger.

Common Gull (p. 154) Slightly larger. Stripey blotches on head in winter.

Common Tern (pp. 66-67) More slender. Black cap. Long tail.

Kittiwake in winter (p. 153) Dark markings on head. Dove-grey wings with black wing-tips.

Common Tern

Adult in summer plumage has short red legs, an orange-red, black-tipped bill that is finer than a gulls', and a black cap

FACT FILE

Scientific name
Sterna hirundo

Family Gulls and Terns (Laridae)

Length 34–37 cm (inc. tail streamers of 5–8 cm)

Wingspan 70–85 cm

Nest Scrape on the ground

Eggs 2–3, creamy, and blotched with black

Broods usually one

Food Small fish

Voice Sharp 'kirrit, kirrit'

Where to see
Summer visitor between April and October to colonies on low-lying coastal sites and off-shore islands. It also breeds on shingle bars and islands on gravel pits. Moves south in winter to west and southern Africa.

The slender elegance and the long forked tail of the Common Tern gives it the local name of 'sea swallow'. It is a long-distance migrant visiting the British Isles to breed and returning each winter to the coasts of Africa, some reaching as far as South Africa. It breeds in colonies around the coast and at inland sites such as gravel pits, where there is suitable habitat.

In winter, adults have a black bill, a white forehead and shorter tail

Juvenile has a gingery back that turns to grey over the winter

Winter adults have shorter tails

In flight summer adult has noticeable long streamers and dark grey wing markings. Inner primaries are translucent

Terns fish by hovering and then suddenly dropping to grab the fish in their bills

LOOK-ALIKES

Arctic Tern in flight in summer **(p. 158)** Primaries all translucent. Very long tail streamers. Totally red bill.

Arctic Tern in summer **(p. 158)** Very short legs. Tail streamers protrude beyond the wings.

Sandwich Tern in flight in summer **(p. 159)** Larger. Shaggy crest. Black bill with yellow tip.

Black-headed Gull in flight **(pp. 64–65)** Higher forehead. Black face. Less slender.

Moorhen

Chick is fluffy with red skin on the head

Adult has slaty grey underparts and head, brown wings, a ragged white line along the edge of the wing when folded, a white inverted 'V' on underside of tail, longish green legs and long toes, and a bright red bill with yellow tip and facial shield

FACT FILE

Scientific name *Gallinula chloropus*

Family Rails and Crakes (Rallidae)

Length 27–31 cm

Wingspan 50–55 cm

Nest Cup of grasses in riverside vegetation

Eggs 5–11, buff spotted with brown

Broods 2–3 per year

Food Seeds, plants, aquatic insects

Voice Several calls including a sharp, explosive 'pli-ip'. High-pitched contact family call

Where to see A resident in the vicinity of small areas of water where there is dense vegetation in which to nest and forage. Northern European breeders move south in winter.

This is a common waterbird that feeds both in the water and on the land. It has notably long toes and its feet are not webbed, which enables it to walk on land, but it also swims well. In some places it may be very secretive, running for cover at the sight of a person, but in other places it is confiding. When disturbed it may submerge itself beneath the water and breathe through its bill protruding just above the surface. In spring, males will vigorously defend their territories.

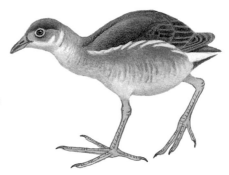

Juveniles have distinct Moorhen shape, but are brown and grey

Toes dangle in flight

When swimming quickly, the head moves back and forth like a clockwork toy

Tail is raised in warning to young

Young of the first brood help to feed young of subsequent broods

LOOK-ALIKES

Coot (p. 160) Larger. Dumpier. White bill and facial shield. Dives readily.

Tufted Duck ♂ (p. 166) Rounded duck-shape. Black and white with tuft.

Tufted Duck ♀ (p. 166) Rounded duck-shape. Brown.

Little Grebe (p. 161) Smaller. Dumpy body. Dives readily.

Mallard

♂ in breeding plumage has metallic bottle green head, yellow bill, narrow white collar, dark brown breast, orange legs and curly tail feathers

FACT FILE

Scientific name
Anas platyrhynchos

Family Ducks, Geese and Swans (Anatidae)

Length 50-60 cm

Wingspan 81-95 cm

Nest Depression in ground lined with twigs, grasses and down

Eggs 9-13, creamy to pale green

Broods 1 per year

Food Seeds, water plants, aquatic invertebrates

Voice Male has a soft, rather nasal, low call and will give a short whistle when courting. It is the male who makes the characteristic quack.

Where to see
Resident throughout western Europe and birds that breed in Scandinavia and eastern Europe move southwards in autumn. Almost every type of water body is used by Mallards. May nest over 1 km from water.

♀ is brown with dark streaking and has orange legs

This is the typical duck. Abundant and widespread, it is the species from which all the domestic varieties (except the Muscovy) have been bred. The brightly coloured drake with his metallic green head, white colour and yellow bill is unmistakable in breeding plumage. However, for a few weeks in late summer he goes into a moult (known as 'eclipse') during which he looks more like the duller female. Mallards pair in autumn, sometimes as early as August. The male sticks close to his mate until she has laid and begun to incubate her clutch the following spring, and then he takes no further part in the breeding process.

♂ in eclipse looks like ♀, but hints of the breeding pattern can often be seen

Duckling has dark brown and yellow down, with yellow tip to bill

In flight, both sexes display a dark blue panel (known as a speculum) on each wing. In straight flight, wings look quite broad and blunt-tipped with fairly quick wing-beats

LOOK-ALIKES

Teal ♂ (p. 164)
About two-thirds the Mallard's size. Dumpy. Green speculum.

Teal ♀ (p. 164)
About two-thirds the Mallard's size. Dumpy. Green speculum.

Wigeon ♀ (p. 165)
Reddish brown. Rounded head. No streaks.

Mallards feed from the surface, by walking on land and by up-ending to reach submerged plants

Shoveler ♂ (p. 162)
Huge bill. White breast.

Great Crested Grebe

Adult in breeding plumage has dark twin tuft and a fringe of face feathers. Note how low the grebe sits in the water

FACT FILE

Scientific name
Podiceps cristatus

Family Grebes (Podicepididae)

Length 46–51 cm

Wingspan 59–73 cm

Nest Mound of plant material floating and anchored to vegetation

Eggs 4, chalky white

Broods 1 or 2 per year

Food Fish

Voice Loud, far-reaching 'ra-ra' calls and a series of nasal sounds and grunts

Where to see Breeds in lakes and large rivers with reeds and other shore-line vegetation. In winter it is found on sea coasts and large lakes.

Its crest and its feather-fringed face make the Great Crested Grebe one of the most extraordinary looking British birds. In early spring the adults perform complex displays involving both members of a pair performing in unison. During the 20th century the population grew with the creation of breeding habitats in the flooded gravel pits left by extraction for the construction industry.

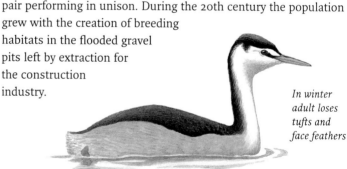

In winter adult loses tufts and face feathers

Juveniles have striped faces and necks

In flight the back looks humped with neck and feet outstretched. White patches give the rapidly whirring wings a flickering appearance

LOOK-ALIKES

Nests are massive mounds of vegetation. When the parent leaves the nest it covers the eggs with vegetation

Complex courtship displays include mutual head-shaking

Mallard ♀ (pp. 70-71) Shorter neck. No contrast between upper and lower parts. Flat bill.

Little Grebe (p. 161) Dumpier. More uniformly coloured.

Coot (p. 160) Black plumage. White facial mask and bill.

When the young are small they will ride on their parent's back

Cormorant (pp. 76-77) Larger. All dark, hooked bill.

Grey Heron

Adult in breeding plumage has a white forehead with yellow bill, a dark patch on the wing and black underparts

Large, long-necked and with long legs, the Grey Heron has a distinctive shape. In its breeding plumage it has a black crest, black patches on the 'elbow' of either wing, a grey back and fine plumes on the breast. The long, strong bill is ideal for coping with its fishy prey. When fishing it stands statue-still. It may also hunt for rodents and frogs in fields using the same method of waiting and striking when the prey comes close.

Juvenile has a grey neck, a dark crown and a dark bill

In flight the neck is folded back and the legs outstretched with toes folded but the feet are noticeable. The wing-beats are slow and not very regular

From above the black primaries contrast with the grey on the wings and back

Herons nest in colonies in trees and adults display to each other when they arrive at and leave nest

When it catches a fish the heron turns it so that it's swallowed headfirst. Once the fish has been swallowed the heron washes its bill

LOOK-ALIKES

Cormorant in flight **(pp. 76-77)** Neck outstretched, shallow wing beats and frequent gliding.

Mute Swan in flight **(pp. 80-81)** Neck outstretched, wings appear to be set back.

Canada Goose in flight **(pp. 78-79)** Neck outstretched, pointed wings.

Common Buzzard in flight **(pp. 50-51)** Fingered wings, fast and stiff wing-beats in direct flight.

75

Cormorant

Adults in breeding plumage have a white patch on either thigh and a brown back with a green metallic sheen

FACT FILE

Scientific name
Phalacrocorax carbo

Family Cormorants and Shags (Phalacrocoracidae)

Length 77-94 cm

Wingspan
121-149 cm

Nest Mound of weed or twigs on cliff or in tree

Eggs 3-4, pale blue

Broods 1 per year

Food Fish

Voice Largely silent, but does make guttural sounds at breeding colonies

Where to see In western Europe Cormorants are largely birds of the coast, although recently they have moved inland and several breeding colonies have been established. After the breeding season the birds disperse but do not undertake massive migration.

The Cormorant's legs are set towards the end of the body, with large webbed feet for propulsion underwater and the long, mobile neck and bill with hooked tip for grasping fish. On land the Cormorant walks with an awkward rolling waddle, but it does manage to perch in trees at inland breeding colonies.

Adult in winter lacks white thigh patches and has greyish face

Juvenile preening. Note pale greyish underparts

Flies in flocks. Note long tail and narrow wings

In flight, the neck is thick and kinked. Note white patch denoting breeding bird

'Spreadeagle' wings drying position is typical. All four toes point forwards

Having successfully caught a fish the Cormorant swallows it headfirst

LOOK-ALIKES

Shag in flight **(p. 168)** Thinner neck. Shorter and more rounded wings.

Shag (p. 168) Dark face. Overall greenish sheen to plumage. No white patch on thigh.

Greylag Goose in flight **(p. 171)** Heavier. More rounded head. Grey on wings.

Gannet immature in flight **(p. 169)** Cigar-shaped. Speckled plumage.

77

Canada Goose

♂ and ♀ look alike and have black heads and necks with white running over much of the head from the chin

FACT FILE

Scientific name
Branta canadensis
Family Ducks, geese and swans (Anatidae)
Length 90–100 cm
Wingspan
160–175 cm
Nest Depression in vegetation lined with grasses and feathers
Eggs 5–6, white
Broods 1 per year
Food Grass, seeds, grain, water plants
Voice Loud, disyllabic honking with the second syllable rising in pitch
Where to see Breeds in marshes, beside lakes and islands in gravel pits. Unlike the Canada Geese native to North America, these feral birds do not migrate, although a population in Sweden moves southwards to avoid frozen water in winter.

This large, long-necked goose was first introduced from North America in the 17th century, but the population exploded in the second part of the 20th century to the extent that Canada Geese have become pests in town parks, farmland and even on wetland nature reserves, where they take over nesting areas of more vulnerable species. Attempts to control numbers have been less than successful. Both parents tend to their young and families stay together into the autumn. The young change from yellow plumage to looking like smaller versions of their parents.

Goslings are covered in yellow down. Yellow fades into grey at about 3 weeks and juveniles gradually become patterned like the adults

In flight the neck is outstretched and the wings are set towards the rear of the body

Outside the breeding season, Canada Geese are seen in flocks

LOOK-ALIKES

Greylag Goose in flight **(p. 171)** Shorter neck. Grey on front of wings. Narrow white 'V' on rump.

Brent Goose in flight **(p. 170)** No white on face.

Mute Swan in flight **(pp. 80-81)** Large. White. Longer neck.

Parents with young are alert to danger and one will almost always be on the look-out

Cormorant in flight **(pp. 76-77)** Pointed wings. Long tail. Longer bill.

From the rear in flight there is a distinct white 'V' on the rump

Mute Swan

FACT FILE

Scientific name
Cygnus olor

Family Ducks, Geese and Swans (Anatidae)

Length 140–160 cm

Wingspan
200–240 cm

Nest Very large mound of vegetation beside water

Eggs 5–7, white

Broods 1 per year

Food Water plants

Voice Do not be misled by its name. The Mute Swan makes a number of sounds, including hissing and snorting. Wing-beats create a throbbing sound as air passes through the feather vanes

Where to see Mute Swans breed on open waters, rivers and ornamental lakes. They have been introduced in several urban areas in Europe. The populations in western Europe are largely sedentary, although flocks of non-breeding birds will move to harbours and other coastal sites.

Very large and usually unafraid of people, the Mute Swan is one of the best known waterbirds. The long neck enables it to feed on underwater vegetation, which it reaches by up-ending. Both sexes have a knob at the base of the bill but the male's is larger. Mute Swans often swim with their wings raised and this is sometimes part of an aggressive display. Flocks of Mute Swans can be seen throughout the year and are composed of non-breeding adults and young birds which have not yet reached breeding condition.

♀ with very young cygnets will sometimes allow them to shelter on her back. Cygnets are grey

In flight, the long neck is outstretched. Wing-beats are deliberate

LOOK-ALIKES

Canada Goose in flight **(pp. 78-79)** Short neck. Black neck.

Greylag Goose (p. 171) Shorter neck. Grey on front of wings. Narrow white 'V' on rump.

Cormorant in flight **(pp. 76-77)** Pointed wings. Long tail. Longer bill.

Grey Heron in flight **(pp. 74-75)** Legs protrude beyond tail. Neck bent back.

The large webbed feet are used as brakes when the swan lands

First-winter birds are brownish-grey with white gradually appearing in late winter and spring

When swans up-end to feed, their feet are used to help their balance

Jackdaw

FACT FILE

Scientific name
Corvus monedula

Family Crows
(Corvidae)

Length 30-34 cm

Wingspan 64-73 cm

Nest Twigs in rock
crevices, in buildings
and in holes in trees

Eggs 4-6, pale blue
spotted with brown

Broods 1 per year

Food Worms, insects,
grain, eggs and
nestlings

Voice Noisy. Using a
variety of calls,
including a sharp
'jyack' and a longer
'kyaar'. Roosting flocks
cackle

Size comparison
Smaller than Carrion
Crow, larger than
Blackbird

Where to see
Jackdaws are found
across Europe (except
for the mountainous
parts of Scandinavia).
Very often in company
with people, nesting in
buildings and woods
and parks with veteran
trees. Resident in most
of its range.

*Jackdaws often
nest in chimneys*

*Wings in flight appear to
be broader and more
pointed than other crows'*

The Jackdaw is the smallest of the 'black' crows. It is a very
sociable bird, often breeding in loose colonies in old buildings
such as castles and cathedrals and is often seen in flocks which
may contain Rooks and other crows. From below, the underwing is
uniformly dark grey. The paler grey nape is often visible on flying
birds and the wings are rather rounded with short 'fingers'. The
eyes are pale grey.

*Juvenile lacks
grey nape*

Rook

In flight there is a noticeable narrowing of the wings as they join the body. Tail is less square than Carrion Crow's

FACT FILE

Scientific name *Corvus frugileus*

Family Crows (Corvidae)

Length 41–49 cm

Wingspan 81–94 cm

Nest Cup-nest of twigs high in trees

Eggs 3–5, pale blue-green blotched with brown

Broods 1 per year

Food Seeds, grain, insects, worms

Voice Very noisy in rookeries with croaks and 'geaah' calls

Population 2.3 million

Size comparison Slightly smaller than Carrion Crow

Where to see Rooks are found wherever there are suitable big trees in which to nest across Britain, except in the most mountainous areas. They are faithful to sites from year to year. Flocks feed in farmland.

The Rook breeds in colonies high in trees, usually near towns or villages, and move into fields to forage. The pale bill and bare patch around the base of the bill give the Rook an intense expression. Rooks have learned that traffic vibration causes worms and other invertebrates to come to the surface of roadside verges, and they can often be seen strutting along the roadside.

Juvenile has dark bill

Nests are built in colonies high in trees

LOOK-ALIKES

Carrion Crow in flight **(pp. 20-21)** Evenly broad wings. Square tail.

Hooded Crow (pp. 20-21) Grey areas better defined, more extensive than Jackdaw.

Carrion Crow (pp. 20-21) Larger. Black.

Starling (pp. 16-17) Smaller. Shaggier.

Jay

The adult has pinkish plumage, streaked forehead, black bill and moustache, black and white wings with blue wing flashes

In flight, the white rump and black on the tail and wings is very noticeable. The wing-beats are slow with a 'rowing' action

FACT FILE

Scientific name
Garrulus glandarius
Family Crows
(Corvidae)
Length 32–35 cm
Wingspan 54–58 cm
Nest Cup of twigs
in tree
Eggs 5–7, buff-
speckled pale green
Broods 1 per year
Food Nuts, acorns,
worms, insects,
nestlings, eggs
Voice Loud, hoarse
screaming call
Size comparison
Slightly smaller than
Wood Pigeon, larger
than Great Spotted
Woodpecker
Where to see Breeds
in coniferous and
deciduous woodland,
and parkland with
mature trees.
Oakwoods are
particularly favoured.
Resident, but young
disperse in late
summer and autumn
when they may be
seen flying over more
open land.

Despite its striking pinkish plumage, black moustache, streaked crest and blue and black wing flashes, this is a member of the crow family. In flight the black tail, white rump and blue wing flashes are unlike any other species. The wings narrow towards the body and its flight appears rather stuttering.

Jays bury acorns and recover them later

LOOK-ALIKES

Magpie (pp. 40–41)
Long tail. Much more
black and white than
jay.

**Great Spotted
Woodpecker
(pp. 42–43)** Smaller
than Jay. Black-and-
white pattern more
complex. Undulating
flight.

In flight, which is gently undulating, the white outer tail feathers and white underwings show

Mistle Thrush

Adult has rounded blotchy speckles, a white breast and white outer tail feathers

FACT FILE

Scientific name
Turdus viscivorus

Family Thrushes and Chats (Turdidae)

Length 26-29 cm

Nest Cup of grasses lined with mud in fork of tree

Eggs 4-5, reddish-spotted blue

Broods 2 per year

Food Insects, worms, berries

Voice Call is often made in flight and is a dry 'zer-r-r-r-r'. Song is Blackbird-like, with short varied phrases delivered loudly and clearly. Often the first bird to sing after a rainstorm

Size comparison Larger than Song Thrush

Where to see Breeds in gardens, open woodland, parks, orchards and farmland with trees. It is largely resident in the British Isles. European visitors to Britain between September and April.

Upstanding and solid-looking, the Mistle Thrush is a large bird compared with the other thrushes. It has more blotchy speckling than the Song Thrush and more pale feathers on the face. In flight there is a large pale patch on either wing and white outer tail feathers. The flight is rather flapping and is less undulating than other thrushes.

Song is delivered from high in trees

LOOK-ALIKES

Song Thrush (pp. 22-23) Smaller than Mistle Thrush. Regular, pointed speckles. Reddish-orange underwing patch.

Fieldfare (p. 87) Close speckles against apricot breast. Grey rump. Reddish brown back.

Redwing (p. 86) Smaller than Mistle Thrush. Pale eyebrow. Reddish underwing patch.

Blackbird ♂ (pp. 18-19) Rounder. Darker.

Redwing

In flight from above the stockier shape separates it from Song Thrush

From below in flight the underwing is rusty red

The facial pattern of the Redwing, with a pale eyebrow and dark stripe through the eye, gives it a distinctive expression. These head markings are an important clue to identification, especially when these thrushes are on the ground and grass may obstruct views of the other diagnostic features. Its name derives from the rusty-red beneath the wing, which shows when the wings are at rest and when in flight.

Redwings feed on hedgerow berries in winter and will move into gardens when the weather becomes very hard

Fieldfare

In flight the underwing is white contrasting with dark primaries, and the tail appears fairly long

From above the pale grey rump is characteristic

Strikingly marked, the Fieldfare is a handsome, rather fierce-looking bird with a grey rump contrasting with a reddish-brown back. The breast is speckled in lines and has an apricot background. A Fieldfare will defend a berry-bearing bush against other birds. It is often seen in flocks with other thrushes, particularly Redwings.

Fallen apples and pears are eaten by Fieldfares and Redwings (at back and front). Berries also provide food for Fieldfares

LOOK-ALIKES

Mistle Thrush (p. 85) Similar size to Fieldfare. Less well-marked.

Song Thrush (pp. 22-23) Slightly larger than Redwing, but smaller than Fieldfare. Less well-marked than either.

Starling in flight **(pp. 16-17)** Chunkier than Redwing. Wings more swept-back.

Song Thrush in flight **(pp. 22-23)** Pale reddish underwing.

Mistle Thrush in flight **(p. 85)** Longish tail. White underwing. White outer tail feathers. Rounded breast.

87

Dunnock

FACT FILE

Scientific name
Prunella modularis
Family Accentors
(Prunellidae)
Length 13-14.5 cm
Wingspan 19-21 cm
Nest Cup in bush
Eggs 4-5, bright blue
Broods 2-3 per year
Food Mainly insects,
but also berries and
seeds
Voice Alarm call is a
sharp 'tih'. Song is a
clear medley of sounds
lasting for about 2
seconds
Size comparison
Similar to Robin
Where to see Breeds
across Europe to
approximately the
latitude of Madrid.
Scandinavian birds
move south in
autumn, but resident
in other parts of
Europe. Favours
gardens, parks, open
woodland and open
areas where there is
plenty of cover.

*Both sexes have grey face
and breast, and streaked
flanks. Back is streaked like
a house sparrow*

*Song is usually
delivered from the
top of a bush or a
tree-branch*

Once known as the 'Hedge Sparrow', the Dunnock is certainly a
bird of hedgerows (and gardens, scrub and open woodland) and
shares the rather drab colouring of the sparrows – but it is not
even closely related to sparrows. It is an insect-eating bird that
tends to skulk and therefore not be noticed, but it is very common.

*Although usually
skulking, Dunnocks
will display by flicking
their wings*

Spotted Flycatcher

Adult is grey with dark back, contrasting with pale front with streaking on forehead and throat

The feeding style is distinctive as the flycatcher chases flying insects and returns to the perch from which it started

FACT FILE

Scientific name
Muscicapa striata

Family Flycatchers (Muscicapidae)

Length 13.5–15 cm

Nest Cup against tree-trunk or wall

Eggs 4–5, pale blue with reddish blotches

Broods 1–2 per year

Food Flying insects

Voice Short, shrill 'zee' call. Song rather high-pitched and scratchy

Size comparison Similar to Robin

Where to see Summer visitor from Africa to almost all of Europe. Breeds in parks, open woodlands and gardens. Has recently become less common.

Despite not being particularly colourful, the Spotted Flycatcher is a very smart little bird. Its pale breast contrasts with its grey head and back. There is subtle streaking on its head and throat which give its rather curious 'spotted' description. It catches flies (and other flying insects) by flying from a perch and returning to the perch. Its posture when perched is upright.

Spotted Flycatchers will nest in open-fronted nestboxes

LOOK-ALIKES

House Sparrow ♂ (pp. 30–31) Much thicker bill. No streaking on flanks.

Robin juvenile **(pp. 24–25)** Rounder, spotted breast. Typical Robin posture.

Pied Flycatcher ♂ (p. 91) Dark brown back contrasts with pale breast. Dumpy. Pale flash on wing.

Redstart ♂ (p. 90) Longish, reddish tail.

Redstart

♀ has pale breast tinged with orange, brown back and wings with rusty-red tail

♂ in summer has rusty-red breast and tail, bluish-grey back and crown, black face, white eye-stripe and forehead

FACT FILE

Scientific name
Phoenicurus phoenicurus

Family Thrushes and Chats (Turdidae)

Length 13–14.5 cm

Nest Cup in hole in tree or wall

Eggs 6–7, pale blue

Broods 2 per year

Food Insects

Voice Whistled 'huit' call, often followed by trisyllabic clicking and light, soft high-pitched, melancholy song

Size comparison Similar to Robin

Where to see Summer visitor found across Europe, but absent from Ireland and more common in the upland woods of Britain.

The red breast and shape of the Redstart are reminiscent of the Robin, but with its red tail and blue-grey back the Redstart is even more striking, but far less confiding. Its favoured habitat is mature deciduous woodland, where it may be surprisingly difficult to see, the striking pattern of the male being effective protective camouflage. The British population has decreased and its status remains of moderate concern.

In flight the rusty-red tail and rump are shown by both sexes

Pied Flycatcher

♂ in summer has white breast, black back and wings with white flashes and white marks on either side of tail

♀ has pale breast, brown back and wings with white flashes

FACT FILE

Scientific name
Fidecula albicilla

Family Flycatchers (Muscicapidae)

Length 12–13.5 cm

Nest Cup in hole in tree or nestbox

Eggs 4–7, pale blue

Broods 1 per year

Food Insects

Voice Call is a quiet clicking and its alarm call is a short, repetitive 'pick'. Its song is loud and consists of 2 second phrases with repetitive elements

Size comparison Similar to Robin

Where to see This little black-and-white bird is found in wooded upland areas in the west and north of Britain, but is absent from Ireland and lowland England. It is a summer visitor that winters in west Africa.

The male of this rather dumpy black and white bird is not very like any other bird found in its woodland habitat. It sits more horizontally than the Spotted Flycatcher, often cocking its tail and raising one wing rather nervously. In autumn, males become more drab and look like females, but the wings and tails are sometimes darker. Pied Flycatchers share their woodland habitat with the Redstart.

Pied flycatchers usually nest in holes, but they will also use next boxes

LOOK-ALIKES

Robin (pp. 23–24) No blue-grey on back. No white on head. Pale mottling on breast.

Great Tit (p. 104) Yellow breast with well-defined black band.

Dunnock (p. 88) Dull colouring. Streaked back. Often feeding on ground.

Chaffinch ♀ (pp. 26–27) Narrower wing-bars.

Stonechat

The female has a reddish breast, streaked head and breast, faint pale eyebrow, white patch on wing

FACT FILE

Scientific name
Saxicola torquata

Family Thrushes and Chats (Turdidae)

Length 11.5–13 cm

Nest Loose cup of grasses and leaves, lined with hair and feathers

Eggs 4–5, pale, bluish

Broods 2–3 per year

Food Small insects and other invertebrates

Voice Call is a shrill, sharp whistle and throaty clicking, but the song is short and high-pitched, rather twittery and monotonous

Size comparison Similar to Robin

Where to see Breeds in open areas with low or poor vegetation, including heathland and moorland with gorse and heather, nesting in low bushes or on the ground. In Britain it is often found in coastal areas, but in Ireland and elsewhere in Europe it is found inland.

Dumpy, short-tailed and with an upright posture, the Stonechat looks rather like a dark-headed robin. The entire head of the male is black and there is a distinct white mark on either side of the neck. The marks on each wing appear as patches where the wings meet the body when the bird is flying. The female has a brown head with a faint pale stripe above the eye and a speckled brown back. In winter, the male's plumage pattern becomes less distinct.

The stonechat will often sit on a prominent perch, looking for its insect prey on the ground, then fly down and snatch the prey

The male appears to be black and white with a red breast

Wheatear

In flight, the white rump and black tail can be seen clearly in both sexes

The male has a blue-grey head and back, a white eyebrow, a black cheek patch and a peachy throat merging to pale underparts

FACT FILE

Scientific name
Oenanthe oenanthe

Family Thrushes and Chats (Turdidae)

Length 14–16.5 cm

Nest In holes in walls, among rocks or burrows

Eggs 5–6, very pale blue, sometimes slightly speckled

Broods 1–2 per year

Food Insects, spiders and small snails

Voice Its call is a whistle or a 'chack'. The song is usually delivered from a perch, such as a boulder, but they may make a song in flight. It's an explosive, fast, hard and chirpy song

Size comparison Slightly larger than Robin

Where to see Wheatears are summer migrants arriving in Britain in late March and April, and leaving in August and September. On migration they may be seen in all types of open areas such as pasture, but they breed in moorland, downland, coastal grassland and high pasture with drystone walls.

Its white rump and short, black-edged tail are the most distinctive characteristics of Wheatears of all ages when they fly (male in flight top right). Note the rather upright stance, and how the black on the tail is in the shape of an inverted 'T'. The striking plumage has the effect of breaking up its outline and camouflaging it among boulders in the open habitat in which it breeds. During the first winter both sexes look like females.

The female has a grey-brown back and lacks cheek patch

LOOK-ALIKES

Bullfinch in flight (p. 94) Black head. ♂ has red breast. Different habitat.

Meadow Pipit (p. 113) White outer tail feathers. Streaked brown. No white on rump.

Yellowhammer (p. 96) White outer tail feathers. Chestnut back. Yellow head.

Linnet (p. 95) White outer tail feathers. Red breast. Grey head.

Chaffinch (pp. 26–27) White outer tail feathers. Wing-bars. Pinkish breast.

Bullfinch

Adult ♂ is compact and has a black cap, a bright red breast, an ash-grey back, black-and-white wings, a white rump and a black tail

FACT FILE

Scientific name
Pyrrhula pyrrhula

Family Finches
(Fringillidae)

Length 15.5–17.5 cm

Nest Raft of fine twigs in trees and bushes

Eggs 4–5, pale blue, purple spotted

Broods 1–2 per year

Food Buds, seeds

Voice Call is a low almost breathy whistling 'phew'. Song is a mixture of low-pitched, squeaky notes with double 'phew-phew' note inserted

Size comparison Similar to Greenfinch

Where to see Mainly resident, breeding across much of Europe in woodlands, parks, large gardens and well-grown hedges.

Adult ♀ is compact and has a black cap, a greyish brown breast, a buffish grey back, black-and-white wings, a white rump and a black tail

The population of this handsome bird has declined, but it is still to be seen in open woodland and hedgerows today. Despite the male's bright plumage, it is an unobtrusive bird and most likely to be noticed when its rump shows in flight. Bullfinches stay in pairs throughout the year and if you see one sex the other is likely to be close by. Each sex has a black cap and stout bill, black-and-white wings and a black-and-white tail.

In flight the grey back, white rump and black tail are very obvious

Linnet

♂ has a red breast, red forehead, grey head and a plain brown back

♀ has a pale breast with a brown-streaked crown and back

FACT FILE

Scientific name
Carduelis cannabina

Family Finches
(Fringillidae)

Length 12.5–14 cm

Nest Cup in bush

Eggs 4–6, pale blue speckled with red

Broods 2–3 per year

Food Seeds

Voice In flight dry, slightly nasal, high-pitched twittering call. Song is a mixture of rattles and musical whistling notes

Size comparison
Similar to Robin

Where to see Breeds in gardens, heaths and open areas with thick vegetation. Resident in much of Europe, but a summer migrant to Scandinavia and eastern Europe, moving south and east in winter.

This restless little finch flies from bush to bush in a bounding fashion. Throughout the summer pairs remain together before joining with others to form a flock which roam the winter countryside in search of food. They will also feed with other finches and sparrows. This is a species that is more common than many people think, but its population is declining.

In flight each sex has white outer tail feathers and small white wing flashes

LOOK-ALIKES

Chaffinch (pp. 26–27)
Grey-blue head. Pinker breast.

Goldfinch (p. 97) Red face. Bright yellow wing flashes.

House Sparrow ♀ (pp. 30–31) Heavier. Pale eye-stripe.

Redpoll (p. 99) Smaller. More delicate. Brown streaked breast.

Stonechat (p. 92) Dumpy. More upright. Black head.

Yellowhammer

The adult ♀ in summer has more dark markings on head and face, a reddish-brown rump and a streaked breast

FACT FILE

Scientific name
Emberiza citrinella

Family Buntings
(Emberizidae)

Length 15.5–17cm

Nest Cup in low bush or hedge

Eggs 3–5, purplish-blotched white

Broods 2–3 year

Food Seeds, berries

Voice Call is a combination of discordant notes. The song is 5–8 short notes that are sometimes represented as 'a-little-bit-of-bread-and-no-cheeeeese'

Size comparison Similar to House Sparrow

Where to see Breeds in well-hedged farmland, woodland edge, heathland and scrubby areas across Europe from northern Spain to Scandinavia. Most Yellowhammers are resident, although the most northerly breeders move south in winter.

The adult ♂ in summer has a yellow head and face, yellow underparts, a reddish-brown rump, a streaked reddish-brown back and a breast suffused with reddish-brown

A male Yellowhammer singing its 'a-little-bit-of-bread-and-no-cheeeeese' from the top of a hedge is one of the special sights and sounds of a British summer. Despite a continuing fall in the population, which is possibly due to intensive farming methods causing a lack of food, it is still a common bird of open countryside and relatively easy to see.

In flight, white outer tail feathers are obvious

In winter, Yellowhammers are often found in flocks with other buntings and finches. In winter ♂ look very like ♀

Goldfinch

Juvenile lacks bold face markings and has striated back and breast, with yellow and black wings

Adult has a longer bill than other finches, a red face, white cheeks, a black cap and nape with yellow and black wings

FACT FILE

Scientific name
Carduelis carduelis

Family Finches (Fringillidae)

Length 12–13.5 cm

Nest Cup of feathers and moss in crown of tree

Eggs 4–7, blue with dark spots

Broods 2 per year

Food Seeds, especially thistles and teasels

Voice Three-syllable skipping call. Song is quiet and trilling

Size comparison Similar to Robin

Where to see Found across Europe north to southern Sweden. Most populations are resident, but eastern and northern breeders migrate south-westwards in autumn. Breeds in gardens, woodland edges, orchards and scrub.

Goldfinches fly in family flocks until they form larger flocks in winter, foraging for food in the countryside and feeding on thistles and teasels

This smart finch was once prized as a cagebird and trapped extensively in the wild. It has benefited from greater protection and is now a common bird in much of Britain, having recently taken to feeding at bird tables.

In flight, the bright yellow flashes on black wings are striking against the white rump and black tail with white markings

LOOK-ALIKES

Greenfinch ♂ (pp. 28–29) Chunky. Yellow wing flashes not extensive.

Linnet ♂ (p. 95) No yellow. Grey head.

Corn Bunting (p. 101) Very stocky build. No yellow.

Reed Bunting ♂ (p. 100) Dark facial markings. No yellow.

Siskin

♀ lacks black on head and throat and yellow on head

Adult ♂ has a green back with black streaks, a black cap and throat, a greenish-yellow breast and yellow on head, pale underparts and yellow bar on wings

FACT FILE

Scientific name
Carduelis spinus

Family Finches
(Fringillidae)

Length 11–12.5 cm

Nest Cup high in
conifer

Eggs 3–5, pale blue
speckled with red

Broods 2 per year

Food Seeds of alder,
spruce and birch

Voice Two two-
syllable calls, one with
a rising second note
and the other with a
descending second
note – 'ti-su' and 'tu-i'.
Song of twittering and
trilling notes

Size comparison
Similar to Blue Tit

Where to see Breeds
in conifers and mixed
woodland, mainly
spruce, in eastern
Europe and
Scandinavia and in
upland forests
elsewhere, including
Britain where most are
winter visitors.

The range of this bird seems to have spread further south in Britain thanks to the increase in garden bird feeding in winter. Peanuts and sunflower seeds in red net bags are attractive to birdtable-visiting Siskins. They are not much larger than Blue Tits and almost as agile when feeding at the end of branches, particularly of spruce, alders and birches.

Flocks of Siskins, often in the company of Redpolls, feed on the seeds of alders

In flight, yellow wing-bars contrasts with dark wings

Redpoll

In spring plumage ♂ has a breast suffused with pinkish-red, a pale eyebrow, a red forehead, a brown back with dark stripes and a tiny black bib (red on breast less obvious in winter)

♀ is similar to ♂, but lacks pinkish-red breast

FACT FILE

Scientific name
Carduelis flammea
Family Finches (Fringillidae)
Length 11.5-14 cm
Nest Cup in tree
Eggs 4-5, pale blue with reddish speckles
Broods 1-2 per year
Food Seeds (especially birch)
Voice Flight call is a harsh metallic 'chett-chett-chett'. Delivers song in flight – a series of metallic calls interspersed with dry reeling 'serrrrrr'
Size comparison Similar to Blue Tit
Where to see Breeds in birch forest, young conifer forests and dense copses in open areas such as heaths. Breeds in Britain and Ireland, Scandinavia and in central Europe. A winter visitor elsewhere in Europe.

In winter this restless little finch forms flocks that rarely stay in one place very long. They feed high in trees, but are also increasingly coming to bird tables. When it feeds on tree seeds it will hang upside down in a rather tit-like manner, often in company with Siskins. Population has declined dramatically.

In flight, whitish rather narrow wing-bars can be seen

LOOK-ALIKES

Linnet ♀ (p. 95)
Larger. Longer tail.

Greenfinch ♂ (pp. 28-29) Larger. Less green than ♂ Siskin and greener than ♀.

Yellowhammer ♂ (p. 96) No green. Larger than both Siskin and Redpoll. Longer tail.

Linnet ♂ (p. 95) Larger. Less striated and with more red than Redpoll. Longer tail.

Blue Tit (pp. 32-33) Much more yellow than Siskin.

Reed Bunting

♂ *in summer has a black head, a black bib, a white moustache joining into white collar around nape, a grey rump and pale striations on back*

♀ *in summer has a dark head, a buff eye-stripe, a striped breast and a white moustache (but white collar)*

FACT FILE

Scientific name
Emberiza schoeniclus

Family Buntings (Emberizidae)

Length 13.5–15.5 cm

Nest Cup of grasses on or near the ground

Eggs 4–5, pale grey with black markings

Broods 2–3 per year

Food Seeds

Voice High, soft 'see-ew' down-slurring final syllable. Song has several simple notes ending in a hurry

Size comparison Similar to House Sparrow

Where to see Breeds across Europe. Northern and eastern breeders move south in autumn. Nests in reedbeds and around lakes and large rivers. In Britain it is a resident, but birds from Scotland and northern England move southwards. In winter Reed Buntings may move away from water and turn up at garden bird tables.

Numbers of the Reed Bunting have been falling in recent years. In spring the male's simple song is heard near freshwater, as he perches on bushes and reeds. Its flight is jerky, uneven and it makes for cover rapidly. Outside the breeding season, the Reed Bunting may be seen feeding in fields with other buntings and finches, and may sometimes venture into gardens in search of food.

In winter ♂ loses black head and white moustache and collar become less well-defined

Corn Bunting

Note how notches can be seen when the bill is open

In flight, which is fairly ponderous, the legs dangle

FACT FILE

Scientific name
Miliaria calandra

Family Buntings
(Emberizidae)

Length 16-19 cm

Nest Cup of plant
material on the ground
in bush

Eggs 4-6, white
spotted with grey

Broods 1-2 per year

Food Seeds, berries

Voice Its call is a
sharp, metallic 'tsritt',
and the song is a brief
repetitive jingling,
delivered from a post,
top of a hedge or
telegraph wire

Size comparison
Slightly smaller than
Skylark

Where to see Breeds
in open farmland
where there are
isolated trees, bushes,
or even telegraph
posts and wires from
which it can sing. In
most places it is
resident.

This is the chunkiest of the buntings and
was once much more common, but has
declined across Europe since the 1960s.
When the male is perched and singing the
rump can sometimes be prominent in
silhouette. Close examination shows that
the Corn Bunting has a notched bill with
which it holds seeds and cracks the husks.

*The adult lacks any really
definitive characteristics
except its bulky shape and
heavy bill*

LOOK-ALIKES

**House Sparrow ♂
(pp. 30-31)** Grey on
head. Black more
blurred.

**House Sparrow ♀
(pp. 30-31)** Buff
eye-stripe. Sparrow-
shaped.

**Yellowhammer ♀
(p. 96)** Less heavy
than Corn Bunting.
Hint of yellow.
Chestnut rump.

Sedge Warbler

The adult has a dark crown contrasting with a well-defined pale eyebrow, stripes down the back and a low forehead

FACT FILE

Scientific name
Acrocephalus schoenobanus

Family Warblers (Sylvidae)

Length 11.5–13 cm

Nest Cup on or near ground

Eggs 5–6, pale green with buff speckles

Broods 1 per year

Food Insects

Voice Sharp 'tsek' call. Song, often delivered in flight, is a not very tuneful cascade of trills and whistles

Size comparison Slightly smaller than Robin

Where to see This summer visitor arrives in Britain and Ireland in April and leaves in mid-September. Breeds across northern Europe in dense vegetation in marshy places, well-vegetated river banks and reedbeds where there are bushes and other plants.

The low forehead with a black crown and buff stripe above the eye, combined with the dark striations on its back, give the Sedge Warbler a rather smart, streamlined appearance. In its wetland habitats it is a common breeding bird. It nests in the drier parts of marshes and river banks where there is plenty of vegetation.

In flight, the rump appears to be a warm yellowish brown

Reed Warbler

The Reed Warbler is agile and perches horizontally on vertical reed stems

FACT FILE

Scientific name
Acrocephalus scirpaceus

Family Warblers (Sylvidae)

Length 12.5–14 cm

Nest Cup of grasses strung between plant stems

Eggs 4, pale green with olive spots

Broods 1 per year

Food Insects

Voice The call is a short, not very noticeable 'che'. The song is a slow nervous song, repeated two or three times and interspersed with whistles

Size comparison Similar to Robin

Where to see The breeding distribution of the Reed Warbler is more southerly than the closely related Sedge Warbler, stretching from the Mediterranean to southern Scandinavia, and including England and Wales. Breeds in reedbeds. Summer migrant from mid-April to September. Winters in sub-Saharan Africa.

It has a sloping forehead, a warm brown back and rich buff underparts

This is one of the species that is often chosen as a host by the Cuckoo for its eggs. The young Cuckoo grows to such a size that by the time it is ready to fly it has outgrown the Reed Warbler's delicate nest strung between the stems of reeds. The Reed Warbler is a subtly-coloured, unobtrusive bird.

The song is delivered from a perch high on a reed stem

LOOK-ALIKES

Willow Warbler (p. 110) Rather greyish green. Smaller. No striations. More rounded head.

Reed Bunting ♀ (p. 100) Thick bill. White 'moustache'. Longish body and tail. **Chiffchaff (p. 111)** Olive green. Smaller. More rounded head.

Garden Warbler (p. 108) Brown. Rounder. No eye-stripe. In drier habitats.

Great Tit

Juvenile has yellow cheeks

In flight, it has white edges to tail, small white bars on wings

The ♂ has a yellow breast with a black stripe that becomes larger towards the underparts, white cheeks and a black cap

FACT FILE

Scientific name
Parus major

Family Tits (Paridae)

Length 13.5-15 cm

Nest Cup of feathers in hole or nestbox

Eggs 8-13, white with red spots

Broods usually 1 per year

Food Insects, seeds

Voice Wide range of calls including 'teacher-teacher-teacher' and repetitive 'che-che-che-che-che...' Simple song that goes up and down

Size comparison Similar to Robin

Where to see From North Africa to Scandinavia and across Europe in woodland and in parks, gardens and orchards.

This favourite garden visitor is a woodland bird, whose egg-laying is dictated by the availability of caterpillars on which to feed its young. In autumn and winter, Great Tits move into gardens in large numbers in search of food. In winter it forages for seeds and invertebrates beneath fallen leaves and crevices in the tree bank.

The ♀ has similar colouring to ♂ but has a less distinct black stripe

Adult has a black crown, a white patch on nape, two wing-bars, a white face and a brown breast (lacks any yellow)

Juvenile (right) has a yellowish breast and face for a few weeks

FACT FILE

Scientific name
Parus ater

Family Tits (Paridae)

Length 10–11.5 cm

Nest Cup in hole

Eggs 7–9, white speckled with red

Broods 2 per year

Food Insects, seeds

Voice Clear 'zee-zee-zee' calls and repeated two-syllable call. Song is very fast and like Great Tit's

Size comparison
Similar to Blue Tit

Where to see Mainly found as a breeding bird in conifers across Europe, but it spreads into the countryside in autumn, when it is most likely to be seen in gardens.

Although lacking any of the yellowness of Blue Tits or Great Tits, the Coal Tit is a perky, attractive little bird. Its head is large and it will raise a small crest when nervous. It has a very fine bill with which it extracts insects from pine needles.

The Coal Tit often flies in flocks with other tits, such as Long-tailed Tits and Blue Tits

LOOK-ALIKES

Blue Tit (p. 32–33)
Small. Blue crown. Black eye-stripe.

Blackcap ♂ (p. 109)
More slender shape. Black cap. High forehead.

Blackcap ♀ (p. 109)
Brown cap.

Long-tailed Tit

No other small bird has such a comparatively long tail, which is used to help balance when it is feeding on tips of branches

In flight short wings, long tail and round body are unlike any other species. The flight is gently undulating

Family flocks of Long-tailed Tits can be seen for most of the year outside the breeding season. The birds in these flocks stay close to each other and the flocks move rapidly through woods, gardens and hedges in search of food. The birds' feeding behaviour seems very restless as they search for tiny insects and they seldom stay anywhere for very long.

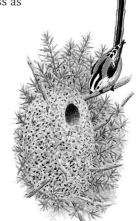

The intricately built dome nest is covered with lichens which can make it difficult to see. It is built from moss held together with gossamer and lined with feathers

Goldcrest

The ♀ has a yellow crest, a white ring around the eye, a small wing-bar and a very fine bill

The ♂ has an orange crest, a white ring around the eye, small wing-bar and a very fine bill

FACT FILE

Scientific name
Regulus regulus

Family Warblers (Sylviidae)

Length 8.5–9.5 cm

Nest Cup of moss and feathers high in tree

Eggs 7–10, white speckled brown

Broods 2 per year

Food Insects

Voice High-pitched, thin, repetitive tri-syllabic 'zi–zi–zi–zi' call. Song is similar but ends in a flourish

Size comparison Similar to Wren

Where to see Breeds in coniferous and mixed woodlands where it chooses conifers such as yews, spruces and firs. Mostly resident.

The tiny Goldcrest is the smallest of European species. Its presence is often betrayed by its high-pitched call as it feeds on insects high in conifers. Its tiny cup nest is built towards the tip of a branch. In winter it may be seen with flocks of tits.

Goldcrests feed high in the canopy by picking insects from the conifer needles and branches

LOOK-ALIKES

Willow Warbler (p. 110) Larger than Goldcrest. No orange or yellow on crest.

Chiffchaff (p. 111) Larger than Goldcrest. No orange or yellow on crest.

Wren (pp. 34–35) Slightly bigger than Goldcrest. Dumpy.

Blue Tit (pp. 32–33) Dumpy. Thicker bill than Goldcrest.

Coal Tit (p. 105) Dumpy. Large head.

Garden Warbler

FACT FILE

Scientific name
Sylvia borin

Family Warblers
(Sylviidae)

Length 13-14.5 cm

Nest Cup nest in bush

Eggs 4-5, white
blotched with brown

Broods 2 per year

Food Insects, berries

Voice Call is a series
of sharp clicking 'chek,
chek, chek, chek',
which becomes more
rapid as the warbler
becomes agitated.
Song lasts from 3-8
seconds, with a
succession of rather
deep notes varying in
pitch to the extent that
it has been described a
'rippling brook'

Size comparison
Similar to Robin

Where to see This
summer migrant
breeds north from
Spain to Scandinavia
and winters in Africa.
Its breeding habitat is
woods with clearings,
well-vegetated
parkland and large
gardens.

*This small bird is basically brown
but has pale underparts, off-white
beneath the rump, a grey smudge
on the side of its neck, thickish
legs and a thickish bill*

The Garden Warbler is the quintessential little brown bird. It is
certainly small and brown: it has no obvious field characters and
its name is accurate only in that it does breed in gardens if they
are very large gardens. It is not
easy to see the Garden Warbler
because of its skulking
nature and it is more
often heard than seen. It
is a sturdy little bird and
more thickset than many
other warblers. It breeds
in woodlands where
there are clearings with
plenty of bushes.

Blackcap

♂ has greyish plumage and a black cap which does not extend to nape

FACT FILE

Scientific name
Sylvia atricapilla

Family Warblers
(Sylviidae)

Length 13.5–15 cm

Nest Cup in bush

Eggs 5, white,
blotched with red

Broods 2 per year

Food Insects, berries

Voice Hard, loud 'tek'
which is repeated
rapidly when the bird
is alarmed. Song
begins in a rather
unsure way, similar to
the Garden Warbler's,
but then becomes
clear and flute-like

Size comparison
Similar to Robin

Where to see Dense
understorey in
woodlands, parks and
large gardens provide
the conditions for
breeding Blackcaps. In
winter it will visit bird
tables. Breeds across
Europe from Spain to
southern Scandinavia.
Summer visitor across
northern and eastern
parts of its range, but
a short- distance
migrant or resident
elsewhere.

Blackcaps feed on berries in autumn

Warmer winters and garden bird tables have changed the habits of Blackcaps in southern Britain, and over the last quarter of the 20th century they became more frequently seen in gardens during the winter. In less than a quarter of century, it has changed from a summer migrant to a resident in parts of Europe, which shows how bird behaviour can evolve very quickly. It is less skulking than the closely related Garden Warbler.

The ♀ has a greyish-brown back, pale brown underparts and a red-brown cap

LOOK-ALIKES

**Willow Warbler
(p. 110)** No cap.
Greenish. Eye-stripe.

Whitethroat (p. 112)
Grey head. White
throat. Brown back.

Chiffchaff (p. 111)
No cap. Greenish.
Eye-stripe.

Dunnock (p. 88)
Streaked brown and
grey.

Coal Tit (p. 105)
Black cap. White nape
patch. Contrast
between grey back and
pale underparts.

Willow Warbler

The adult has an olive head and back, a well-defined eyebrow and pale legs

FACT FILE

Scientific name
Phylloscopus trochilus

Family Warblers
(Sylviidae)

Length 11–12.5 cm

Nest Domed nest on
the ground

Eggs 6-7, white with
reddish speckles

Broods 1-2 per year

Food Insects

Voice Soft two-
syllable 'huitt' call.
The song is a sweet,
soft whistling,
descending 3-second
verse which is
frequently repeated

Size comparison
Slightly larger than
Blue Tit

Where to see Nests
in all types of
woodland, gardens,
parks and copses. It is
a summer migrant, in
Britain from April until
September, when it
moves south to
tropical Africa.

Willow Warblers and Chiffchaffs are very similar species who belong to a genus of warblers known as leaf warblers, because of their habit of feeding high in the tree canopy on insects. Both species nest on the ground. The voices of the two species are very distinctive, but they can be distinguished visually if you have a good view. The Willow Warbler's song is a series of falling notes and its call is a soft 'huitt'.

In autumn juveniles have an extensive yellow breast

Chiffchaff

Short eyebrows are less well-defined than the Willow Warbler's

The adult has a greyish green back, buffish white underparts, dark legs and a short eyebrow which is less well-defined than Willow Warbler's

FACT FILE

Scientific name
Phylloscopus collybita

Family Warblers (Sylviidae)

Length 10–12 cm

Nest Dome on ground

Eggs 4–9, white with purple speckles

Broods 1–2 per year

Food Insects

Voice Call is a soft whistled, slightly upslurred 'huitt'. Song is a slow, repeated 'chiff-chaff'

Size comparison Slightly larger than Robin

Where to see Breeds in open woodland with tall deciduous trees and some shrub layer. Most Chiffchaffs seen in Britain are summer visitors, which winter in the southern Mediterranean and south of the Sahara. Some Chiffchaffs breeding in Scandinavia may winter in the British Isles.

The Chiffchaff really is much more likely to be seen than heard. Its two-syllable song in late March and April is one of the welcome sounds that heralds spring. It sings throughout the summer. Looks very similar to the Willow Warbler, but is less well-marked or well-coloured.

Chiffchaffs feed on insects on the ground and at the end of leaves

LOOK-ALIKES

Goldcrest (p. 106)
Tiny. Orange and yellow crest.

Wren (pp. 34–35)
Tiny. Stubby tail. Perky stance.

Garden Warbler (p. 108) Larger. Brown.

Whitethroat (p. 112) Grey head. White throat. Brown back.

Whitethroat

In flight, the white outer tail feathers can be seen clearly

FACT FILE

Scientific name
Sylvia communis

Family Warblers (Sylviidae)

Length 13–15 cm

Nest Cup in bush close to the ground

Eggs 4–5, pale blue with olive speckles

Broods 2 per year

Food Insects, berries

Voice Call is a hoarse 'tac, tac' and a brief, fast, frequently repeated, rather scratchy sound is delivered from a perch. When it has a song-flight the song becomes more fluid

Size comparison Similar to Robin

Where to see A summer visitor, arriving in Britain and Ireland in May and leaving in August. Breeds in scrub, farmland, hedges, and open woodland. Winters south of the Sahara.

♂ has a grey head, a white throat, buff breast, rusty wings, a long tail with white outer tail feathers and buffish legs

Although not colourful, the male Whitethroat is one of the more strikingly patterned warblers. The soft grey of the head merges into the brown back and contrasts with the white throat. This is a sturdy bird which appears to move more clumsily than its smaller relatives. It often chooses a perch high in a bush from which to sing but it may also sing in flight.

♀ has a brown head, buff breast, rusty wings, a long tail with white outer tail feathers and buffish legs

Meadow Pipit

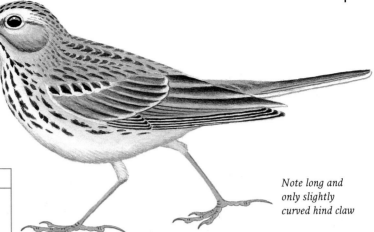

Note long and only slightly curved hind claw

The Meadow Pipit lives much of its life on the ground, but will perch on fences, posts and isolated trees

FACT FILE

Scientific name
Anthus pratensis

Family Wagtails and Pipits (Motacillidae)

Length 14–15.5 cm

Nest Cup on ground

Eggs 3–5, with variable background and brown spots

Broods 2 per year

Food Insects, seeds

Voice Flight call is a high, thin 'ist-ist-ist'. Song delivered in flight is a series of rapidly repeated notes that change several times

Size comparison Smaller than Skylark

Where to see Breeds in open country including moorland, heaths, pastures and bogs. Resident in British Isles and northern Europe. Other populations migrate to British Isles and elsewhere in Europe in winter.

Small, brown and easily overlooked, the Meadow Pipit is one of the commoner British birds. It is a bird of open country, often seen in small groups and identified by its distinctive call. It most closely resembles the Skylark, but is smaller and has no crest. Its flight appears rather weak at first but is gently undulating once it is underway.

White outer tail feathers show in flight

LOOK-ALIKES

Skylark (pp. 36–37) Larger and stockier. Slight crest. Broader wings.

Blackcap ♀ (p. 109) Brown cap. No streaks.

Dunnock (p. 88) Grey face. Darkish brown and grey. Streaked.

Garden Warbler (p. 108) Pale throat. No streaks.

Corn Bunting (p. 101) Stocky. Thick bill.

Grey Wagtail

♂ has a yellow breast, a blue-grey back, a yellow rump, a black throat and a white eye-stripe and moustache

♀ has similar pattern as ♂ but is paler

FACT FILE

Scientific name
Motacilla cinerea

Family Wagtails and Pipits (Motacillidae)

Length 17-20 cm

Nest Cup in crevice near water

Eggs 4-6, buff with greyish mottling

Broods 1 per year

Food Insects

Voice Sharper and higher version of Pied Wagtail's call. Song is a series of short 'ziss' notes

Size comparison Similar to Pied Wagtail

Where to see Found beside fast-flowing upland streams and by mill ponds and locks on slower rivers. The British and Irish populations are resident, but may be joined in winter by migrants from Europe.

This is the most elegant of the three British breeding wagtails. It is slender and graceful and almost always associated with water. It breeds near fast-flowing water in upland streams, near mill-races and around weirs, but may occasionally visit gardens with large ponds in autumn or winter. Its tail seems larger than those of the other two wagtails.

In flight, the Grey Wagtail shows a yellow-green rump, a long tail with white outer feathers and distinct white wing-bars

Yellow Wagtail

♂ has a yellow face, a sulphur yellow breast, a greenish back and a long tail that flicks up and down

FACT FILE

Scientific name
Motacilla flava

Family Wagtails and Pipits (Motacillidae)

Length 15-16 cm

Nest Depressed cup in ground

Eggs 5-6, greyish brown-speckled

Broods 1-2 per year

Food Insects

Voice Call is a loud 'see-ip'. Song is a mere two rather scratchy notes

Size comparison Slightly smaller than Pied Wagtail

Where to see Breed across Europe from Wales eastwards. They are birds of wet meadows and other marshy areas, such as the edges of lakes and sewage farms. The yellow-headed Yellow Wagtail is the race that is found in England and Wales. They are summer visitors from April to September and they winter in Africa.

Once a common sight in wet meadows, feeding among the grazing cattle and nesting in hoof-prints in the grass, the Yellow Wagtail's numbers have declined as its riverside habitat has become drier. Its insect food has declined over the last quarter of the 20th century due to changes in farming practice. Across Europe there are several races of this species and they can be identified by the different colours and patterns of their heads.

♀ has a darker face, a yellow-green back and a long tail that flicks up and down

LOOK-ALIKES

Pied Wagtail ♀ (pp. 38-39) Greyish colouring. No yellow.

Pied Wagtail ♂ (pp. 38-39) Black, white and grey. No yellow.

Yellowhammer ♂ (pp. 96) Streaked plumage. Stockier shape. More upright stance.

Kingfisher

♀ has a red base to lower mandible

♂ has a black bill, a bright blue back contrasting with blue-green wings and head, an orange breast, orange cheeks and a white throat

The juvenile has pale tip to bill

FACT FILE

Scientific name
Alcedo atthis
Family Kingfishers (Alcedidae)
Length 17-19.5 cm
Wingspan 24-26 cm
Nest Tunnel in river bank
Eggs 6-7, white
Broods 2 per year
Food Fish
Voice Call is short, sharp whistled 'zii'
Size comparison Slightly smaller than Starling
Where to see Breeds south from southern Sweden. Eastern European populations move south and west in autumn. Some Mediterranean breeders move to coasts in winter. Feeds in slow-flowing rivers and sometimes on lakes. Rarely seen far from water.

This splendidly coloured bird looks startling, but it can be extremely difficult to see when perched in a tree in which some leaves are brown, because its breast colour acts as camouflage. Its whistling call is often the first signal of its presence, before one catches a glimpse of its bright blue rump in its swift, direct flight low over the water.

Kingfishers fly swiftly and low over the water. Fish are caught after diving from a perch or hovering above the water

Swift

The Swift is dark brown and has long wings in a crescent

Swifts often fly in tight flocks, rising high to feed on flying insects

FACT FILE

Scientific name
Apus apus

Family Swifts (Apodidae)

Length 16–18 cm

Wingspan 40–44 cm

Nest Pile of plant material in building

Eggs 3, white

Broods 1 per year

Food Flying insects

Voice Shrill, screaming call, often made in chorus by birds flying in tight flocks low over roofs

Size comparison Smaller than Starling (but with longer wingspan), but larger than Swallow

Where to see Swifts breed across Europe. They are summer residents which arrive in May and leave in August to winter in southern Africa.

The air really is the element of the Swift, which only lands at its nest site. Its legs are so short that it cannot take off upwards from a flat surface. Instead it drops from its nesting site high in buildings, so that it has no need of lift. However, once in the air it flies with speed and directness. Feeding, sleeping, and mating among Swifts all take place in the air.

Spaces beneath roofs provide the Swift with nesting places

LOOK-ALIKES

Swallow (pp. 44–45) Metallic royal blue back and wings. Longer tail streamers.

House Martin (p. 118) Forked tail. White rump. Dark blue back and wings.

117

House Martin

FACT FILE

Scientific name
Delichon urbica

Family Swallows and Martins (Hirundinidae)

Length 13.3–15 cm

Nest Mud cup beneath the eaves with a small entrance hole

Eggs 4–5, white

Broods 2–3 per year

Food Flying insects

Voice Twittery calls are made frequently at colonies. The song is a sweet collection of unrelated notes

Size comparison Smaller than Swallow

Where to see This summer visitor is a common species of villages and small towns, where there are nesting sites and open country for it to feed on flying insects. There must also be a supply of mud for nest-building.

In flight the white rump contrasts with the glossy dark blue, almost black, tail and wings. Note the short, forked tail

From beneath the House Martin looks pale with a white breast and no dark breast band. It often glides

In April, the House Martin returns to Europe from Africa to breed, before moving south again in September. Because it breeds in loose colonies nesting beneath the eaves of houses, the House Martin is more familiar to many people than the closely related Swallow. The nest is made of small pieces of mud stuck to the wall and the eaves. The mud is collected from puddles and river banks. It perches in flocks on telegraph wires once its young have fledged.

House Martins are only seen on the ground in early spring, when they collect mud in their bills for nest-building

Sand Martin

The adult has brown wings and tail, a shallowly forked tail and a well-defined brown breast band

FACT FILE

Scientific name
Riparia riparia

Family Swallows and Martins (Hirundinidae)

Length 12-13 cm

Wingspan 26-29 cm

Nest Hole excavated up to 1 m into a bank

Eggs 4-5, white

Broods 2 per year

Food Flying insects

Voice Dry, rasping, repetitive call made when birds are excited at a colony

Size comparison Smaller than Swallow

Where to see
A summer visitor arriving from west Africa in late March and April, leaving in September and early October. The Sand Martin breeds in colonies in sand and earth banks of rivers and gravel pits.

Flocks of Sand Martins hunting flying insects are a feature of open areas of water where there are suitable nesting banks. Their flight is rapid and light. In the late summer and early autumn large flocks build up and will roost in huge numbers in reed beds before their migration to Africa.

Sand Martins nest in colonies, with many holes excavated in a bank

LOOK-ALIKES

Swift in flight **(p. 117)** Larger. Almost totally dark appearance.

Swallow in flight **(pp. 44-45)** Forked tail with streamers. Dark blue back and wings. Dark breast band.

Starling in flight **(pp. 16-17)** Straighter edge to trailing edge of wings. No notch on tail. Stocky. Also sits on telegraph wires.

Lesser Spotted Woodpecker

♀ lacks the red cap

The flight is undulating

♂ has a red cap, a white face leading to its breast without interruption, white bars on the wings, faint streaks on the breast and no red under the tail

FACT FILE

Scientific name
Dendrocops minor

Family Woodpeckers (Picidae)

Length 14–16 cm

Wingspan 24–29 cm

Nest Hole in tree

Eggs 4–6, white

Broods 1 per year

Food Insects and other invertebrates

Voice Short, sharp repeated 'kee-kee-kee-kee' call. Song is a series of 8–15 piping notes. Its drumming is weaker but longer than Great Spotted Woodpecker's (see p. 42), lasting for 1.2–1.18 seconds

Size comparison
Similar to Starling

Where to see
Deciduous woodlands, orchards, parkland, large gardens and alder woodland in river valleys provide the breeding habitat of this resident. Numbers have fallen in recent years and there is concern about its status. Not found in Ireland, Scotland or much of northern England.

This is the smallest of European woodpeckers, Starling-sized but with a distinctive woodpecker shape as it searches for food on branches and tree trunks. The bill is quite short and the forehead rather high. In its undulating flight the typical woodpecker's broad, fingered wings and pointed tail can be clearly seen.

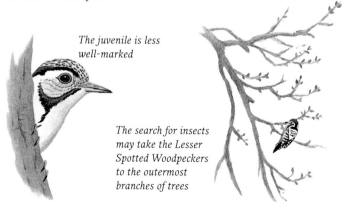

The juvenile is less well-marked

The search for insects may take the Lesser Spotted Woodpeckers to the outermost branches of trees

Green Woodpecker

The ♀ has a completely black moustache

The juvenile is spotted but can still be sexed by the presence or absence of red on the moustache

FACT FILE

Scientific name
Picus viridus

Family Woodpeckers (Picidae)

Length 30–36 cm

Wingspan 45–51 cm

Nest Hole in tree trunk

Eggs 5–7, white

Broods 1 per year

Food Insects, including ants and beetles

Voice Shrill, far-carrying laughing call, which also provides the basis of the song which has a series of 10–18 notes with acceleration of the last few

Size comparison
Similar to Kestrel

Where to see Absent from the north of Scotland and Iceland. Breeds in open deciduous and mixed woodland, parkland, large gardens and commons with trees.

On the ground, the Green Woodpecker has a rather upright stance due to its stiff tail feathers. ♂ has a red centre to its moustache

The Green Woodpecker is most often seen in flight or feeding on the ground of lawns, glades and meadows near woods. It has an extremely long tongue which can probe deep into rotten wood or earth in search of beetle larvae or ants, which adhere to its bristly tip.

Its laughing call carries a long way

The Green Woodpecker's flight is undulating and it closes its wings completely on the downward undulation

LOOK-ALIKES

Great Spotted Woodpecker (pp. 42–43) Smaller than Green Woodpecker. Bold black-and-white marking.

Nuthatch (p. 122) Small. Ashy back. Orange underparts. Square-ended tail.

Treecreeper (p. 123) Brown streaked back. Pale underside. Down-curved bill.

Nuthatch

In flight, the wings are broad. Short flight from tree to tree is direct, but longer flights are undulating

FACT FILE

Scientific name
Sitta europaea

Family Nuthatches
(Sittidae)

Length 12–14.5 cm

Nest In tree hole,
or nestbox with mud
plastered around
entrance

Eggs 6–9, white with
reddish spots

Broods 1 per year

Food Seeds, nuts,
insects

Voice Loud call
sharper than a tit's or
very loud 'twett'. The
song is loud, trilling or
whistling and delivered
from a high perch

Size comparison
Similar to House
Sparrow

Where to see Breeds
in mature trees in
mixed and deciduous
woodlands, parks and
gardens. Not found in
Ireland or Scotland. Is
not uncommon
throughout most of
Europe.

The Nuthatch has a distinctive outline with a long pointed bill, a large head (with no apparent neck), a short square-ended tail and a black eye-stripe

This is a busy and sometimes aggressive bird that can be a delight for those lucky enough to have them as garden visitors. It will visit bird-tables and peanut holders and aggressively defend these from other species. If the entrance to a nest-hole is too big it will use a plaster of mud to reduce the size. It is able to move headfirst down a tree trunk and will hack open nuts it has wedged in crevices with its beak.

The Nuthatch is able to descend tree trunks headfirst, and will wedge nuts in a crevice in order to crack them open

Treecreeper

The dark brown, patterned back contrasts with the plain, pale underside. Usually seen in an upright posture on tree trunks and branches

FACT FILE

Scientific name
Certhia familiaris

Family Treecreepers
(Certhidae)

Length 12.5–17 cm

Nest Cup nest behind loose bark

Eggs 6, white with reddish speckles

Broods 1–2 per year

Food Insects

Voice Call is a repeated buzzing 'tsee-tsee'. Song is high and 2–3 seconds long

Size comparison Similar to House Sparrow

Where to see Breeds in woods, often where there are conifers. In mainland Europe, the more easterly and northerly breeders may move south in winter.

The Treecreeper is equally well adapted to living in trees. Its slightly down-curved bill is used to probe tree bark in search of insects, spiders and other invertebrates. It is less agile than the Nuthatch and can only ascend a tree trunk, needing to fly down to the foot of a trunk and climb upwards, spiralling rather jerkily around the trunk.

The Treecreeper spirals up the tree-trunk and then flies down to the foot of the tree or to another tree

LOOK-ALIKES

Great Tit (p. 104)
Yellow breast. Stripe down chest.

Lesser Spotted Woodpecker (p. 120)
Black and white. Barred pattern on back.

Spotted Flycatcher (p. 89) Sits in upright posture on a perch. Catches insects in flight.

Wren (pp. 34–35)
Dumpier. Smaller. Moves horizontally rather than vertically.

Collared Dove

In flight, the underside of the tail has dark markings at the top of the tail

FACT FILE

Scientific name
Streptopelia decaocto

Family Pigeons
(Columbidae)

Length 31–34 cm

Wingspan 48–56 cm

Nest Platform of twigs
on a branch

Eggs 2, white

Broods 2–5 per year

Food Seeds, grain

Voice Song is a
repeated three-syllable
'coo' with the
emphasis on the
drawn-out second
syllable

Size comparison
Smaller than Wood
Pigeon, larger than
Blackbird

Where to see They
breed in farmyards,
parks and gardens
wherever there are
trees dense enough for
them to nest in. In
winter they are often
founds in flocks
feeding in farmyards
and at harbours where
grain is loaded.
Distribution is across
Europe from northern
Spain to the coast of
Norway.

The adult has soft grey-brown plumage, dark wing-tips, a dark collar on nape fringed with white, red legs and red eyes

Until 1953 the Collared Dove had not been seen in the wild in Britain. Since the 1930s this dove had moved north-westwards across Europe to reach the British Isles and over the next 50 years it became one of the commonest birds in the country, although it seems to have begun to decline slightly. The breeding season is prolonged, and nesting Collared Doves may be found from February to November.

Feeding on the ground, Collared Doves may start to display to each other

Turtle Dove

The adult has tortoiseshell-patterned wings, a pinkish breast, four black marks fringed with white on the neck, black pupil surrounded with orange and eyes ringed with red

FACT FILE

Scientific name
Streptopelia turtur

Family Pigeons (Columbidae)

Length 25-27 cm

Wingspan 49-55 cm

Nest Platform of twigs on a branch

Eggs 2, white

Broods 2 per year

Food Seeds

Voice Song is a deep purring, repeated several times and sounds rather like the ringing tone of a British telephone – 'tur-tur'. It also makes a noisy wing clattering

Size comparison Slightly larger than Blackbird

Where to see The Turtle Dove returns from sub-Saharan Africa in May and stays until August. It is found across Europe, but is absent from Ireland, Scotland and Scandinavia. Open deciduous woodland, copses, well-vegetated parkland and farmland with plentiful trees and scrub.

In flight the tail is more pointed than the Collared Dove's, and the black on the tail contrasts with its white edging

The call of this migrant has been one of the sounds of the English farmland in summer, but in recent years its numbers have declined significantly. It is more often heard than seen, because it tends to keep to dense bushes and trees. Its name is onomatopoeic, deriving from its repetitive, two-syllable call.

LOOK-ALIKES

Wood Pigeon (pp. 46-47) Large. Rotund. Small head. White collar. Predominantly dove-grey.

Stock Dove (p. 127) No collar. Slightly larger. Greyer.

Feral Pigeon (p. 126) Larger. More thickset.

Kestrel ♂ (pp. 48-49) Long tail. Hooked bill. Predominantly brown.

Cuckoo in flight (p. 128) Banded breast. Long tail. Down-curved bill.

Adults will often perch together and mutually preen

Feral Pigeon

FACT FILE

Scientific name
Columba livia
Family Pigeons
(Columbidae)
Length 29-35 cm
Wingspan 60-68 cm
Nest Sparse plant
material on ledge
Eggs 2, white
Broods 2-3 per year
Food Seeds, grain
Voice 'Coos' with
three syllables and
stress on second
Size comparison
Smaller than Wood
Pigeon
Where to see
Although Rock Doves
are confined to the
remoter cliffs of the
western parts of the
British Isles, the Feral
Pigeon is found in
towns throughout the
country. Flocks of
pigeons in fields in
winter may well have
Feral Pigeons among
the Wood Pigeons and
Stock Doves.

*Feral Pigeons
come in a variety
of plumages*

The Feral Pigeon (the one that people used to feed in Trafalgar Square) is extremely common in urban centres while its wild progenitor is now found only in the remotest cliffs. For the pigeon the sheer faces of city buildings with convenient breeding ledges are urban cliffs. Pigeons have been domesticated for thousands of years as a source of food, especially in winter, to enliven winters of salt meat. Feral Pigeons now add a bewildering variety of plumages, from white to almost black, to our bird life. The wild Rock Dove, from which Feral Pigeons have bred, has a white patch on its rump.

*In flight the wings
appear more
pointed than the
Wood Pigeon's or
Collared Dove's*

Stock Dove

Note the black markings that can be seen when the wings are closed

The adult is smaller than the Wood Pigeon and has metallic green markings on the sides of the neck. The vinous colouring on the breast does not extend as far as it does on the Wood Pigeon

In flight the wing-tips are clearly outlined in black, giving them a rather pointed look

FACT FILE

Scientific name
Columba oenas
Family Pigeons (Columbidae)
Length 28–32 cm
Wingspan 60–66 cm
Nest In hole in tree or rocks
Eggs 2, white
Broods 2–3 per year
Food Seeds, grain
Voice Two-syllable 'coo' with weak start and rather monotonous.
Size comparison Smaller than Wood Pigeon
Where to see This is a bird of woodland edge, parkland with mature trees and farmland with hedges and mature trees to provide nesting places. Resident in the west and south, but eastern European populations move westwards in autumn.

Many people overlook this pigeon, but it is quite common and, once you know it, not difficult to differentiate from the Feral Pigeon and Wood Pigeon, with which it may sometimes be seen feeding in farmland in winter. The name is derived from the Old English word 'stock' meaning a tree trunk and referring to this dove's habit of nesting in large holes in trees.

Stock Doves often feed on the ground in small flocks, sometimes with other species of pigeon

LOOK-ALIKES

Wood Pigeon (pp. 46–47) Plumper. Larger. White marks on neck. White wing markings.

Collared Dove (p. 124) Grey-brown. More slender. Black neck markings.
Turtle Dove (p. 125) Smaller. More slender. Mottled pattern on back.
Cuckoo (p. 128) Long tail. Down-curved bill. Barred breast.

Cuckoo

In flight the wingbeats are steady and the wings are not raised higher than the back. The tail has a diamond-shaped tip

The Cuckoo chooses prominent perches, such as telegraph poles, fenceposts and wires. Note the breast with narrow grey lines and small head

Everyone can recognise the male Cuckoo's call, but fewer can recognise the bird itself. The Cuckoo arrives in April and the adults leave in August followed by the young which find their way south to Africa on their own. Few Cuckoos remain in Europe in September. The long pointed wings, long tail and swift direct flight in which the wings are not raised above the horizontal give the impression of a predator in flight, but the head with its slightly down-curved bill is quite unlike that of a bird of prey. Each female tends to specialise in a particular species of host and her eggs imitate theirs.

Young Cuckoos are most likely to be seen when they are being fed by their foster-parents (in this illustration, a Dunnock). They are brownish at this stage

Hobby

The perched Hobby shows smart dark grey and white plumage, with a dark face and 'moustache' and reddish 'trousers'. At rest the wing-tips extend as far as the end of the tail

FACT FILE

Scientific name
Falco subbuteo

Family Falcons (Falconidae)

Length 29-35 cm

Wingspan 70-84 cm

Nest Old crow's nest high in a tree

Eggs 2-3, reddish speckles on yellowish background

Broods 1 per year

Food Flying insects, small birds

Voice Repeated 'kew-kew' call or a high-pitched 'ki-ki-ki'

Size comparison Slightly smaller than Kestrel

Where to see Breeds across Europe south from lowland England, where it is particularly associated with heathland, and southern Scandinavia in areas where there are trees and open country in which to hunt. A summer visitor from late April to September, which migrates to Africa.

This small falcon specialises in hunting small birds and large insects which are caught in flight in its talons. The hunting of the Hobby is dramatic because the bird will swoop down at great speed to snatch its prey in its talons. It is often seen hunting dragonflies on summer evenings and will tear off the insect's wings before consuming the rest of the insect in flight.

In flight the Hobby has a rather Swift-like silhouette. Here, it is chasing a House Martin

LOOK-ALIKES

Kestrel ♂ (pp. 48-49) Grey head. Tan back. Grey tail.

Kestrel ♀ (pp. 48-49) Brown, barred back and tail.

Turtle Dove (p. 125) Mottled back. White on tail.

Collared Dove (p. 124) Grey-brown. Black collar. White on tail.

Swift (p. 117) Body darker. Smaller.

Sparrowhawk (p. 131) Rounded wings.

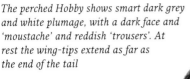

Red Kite

Perched, the Red Kite looks rather scruffy, but it is elegant in flight with its greyish white head. Note the forked tail

Re-introduction programmes in England and Scotland have extended the range of the Red Kite whose British population had been confined to Wales for almost a century. This bird of prey has long wings and a tail with a distinct 'V' in it. It soars and flies directly in a rather lazy way.

Note the white patches on the underside of the long wings and the forked red tail in flight. The wings are often flexed to give a bent appearance

Sparrowhawk

Adult ♀ has slate grey back and rufous barred breast

Adult ♂ has grey brown plumage with fine bars across the breast and pale-eye-stripe. The bands on the tail are sparse

FACT FILE

Scientific name
Accipiter nisus

Family Hawks and Eagles (Accipitridae)

Length 29-35 cm

Wingspan 70-84 cm

Nest Raft of twigs in a tree

Eggs 4-5, white with dark brown blotches

Broods 1 per year

Food Birds

Voice Largely silent except for during the breeding season when it makes a chattering 'keek-keek-keek'

Size comparison Similar to Kestrel

Where to see Breeds in woodland, forests, parks and farms with dense stands of trees, and will visit gardens in urban areas.

Females are larger than males, which enables each sex to exploit prey of a different size. The male tends to take sparrows, finches and similarly-sized birds, while the female will take birds up to the size of doves. Unusually for birds of prey, the sexes have distinctive plumages. This is a dashing predator, flying fast over a short distance and using its long tail to manoeuvre among branches.

In flight the wings appear rounded and the 'fingers' may be seen. ♂ is larger than ♀ which has reddish breast and grey back

LOOK-ALIKES

Kestrel (pp. 48-49) Pointed wings. Hovers.

Buzzard (p. 50) Broad, rounded wings. Short tail.

Wood Pigeon (pp. 46-47) Small head. Deep chest. Rapid wing-beats. (Surprisingly confusing.)

Cuckoo (p 128) Pointed, curved back wings. Small head. Pointed bill.

Barn Owl

The Barn Owl has a heart-shaped face with black eyes and longish, feather-covered legs

FACT FILE

Scientific name
Tyto alba
Family Barn Owls
(Tytonidae)
Length 33–39 cm
Wingspan 80–95 cm
Nest Hole in tree or
building
Eggs 4–7 white eggs
Broods 1–2 per year
Food Small mammals,
small birds, frogs
Voice The call of the
female is a purring
shriek. The alarm call
given in flight is a
shrill squeal, and the
song is an extended
rattling shriek lasting
a couple of seconds
Size comparison
Similar to Kestrel,
larger than Little Owl
Where to see Barn
Owls need open areas
in which to hunt, and
trees or buildings in
which to nest. They
are found throughout
much of Europe, but
not Scandinavia.

Although it is not as common as it once was, the Barn Owl is much more likely to be seen than the Tawny Owl, because of its habit of hunting over fields and roadside verges at dawn and dusk. Its pale plumage and silent flight give this owl a ghostly appearance. It hunts by flying slowly up and down open areas, dropping on unsuspecting mice and voles.

In flight the Barn Owl's head is prominent and it often has traili legs. Note how pale it looks

Tawny Owl

FACT FILE

Scientific name
Strix aluco
Family Owls (Strigidae)
Length 37–43 cm
Wingspan 81–96 cm
Nest Hole in tree or building
Eggs 2–4, white
Broods 1 per year
Food Small mammals, small birds, large insects
Voice The call is a shrill, repeated 'kewick' stressing the final syllable. The song is a mournful hooting that starts with a drawn out falling note, followed by a pause of about 4 seconds, and then a rapid series of drawn-out notes – 'hoooouh, hoo, hoo, hoo, hooooouh'. ♂ has wailing variation of this song
Size comparison Slightly larger than Kestrel
Where to see Absent from Ireland and much of Scandinavia the Tawny Owl is widespread across Europe in forests, well-wooded parkland, gardens and town parkland with mature trees, especially oaks.

The adult has a large rounded head, black eyes, pale stripes on the crown and a pale broken bar on the closed wings

Its completely nocturnal hunting makes the Tawny Owl difficult to see. It may be glimpsed in car headlights or when it has been disturbed during the day. Sometimes the attentions of small birds mobbing a roosting owl during the day provides an opportunity. The song of the Tawny Owl is the traditional owl sound of 'twit-twoo'.

The juvenile is downy grey. If you find one perched in a tree, leave it alone, the parents will be close and will feed it at night

LOOK-ALIKES

Little Owl (pp. 52–53) Small. Squat appearance.

Sparrowhawk ♀ (p. 131) Fingered wings. Long tail. Smaller head.
Kestrel ♀ (pp. 48–49) Pointed wing. Long tail spread when hovering.
Pheasant ♀ (pp. 54–55) Shorter wings. Long neck. Long tail.

Grey Partridge

Adult ♀ looks like ♂ but is duller and has a smaller belly patch

Adult ♂ has an orange-brown face, a grey neck and breast and a dark reddish brown patch on belly

FACT FILE

Scientific name
Perdix perdix
Family Pheasants and Partridges (Phasianidae)
Length 28-32 cm
Nest On ground
Eggs 10-20, buff
Broods 1 per year
Food Seeds, insects, leaves
Voice Sharp triple call as a flock takes to the air. The song of both sexes is hoarse, clipped 'kirr-ik'
Size comparison Slightly smaller than Wood Pigeon
Where to see Breeds in open farmland with shelter in hedges and copses across Europe from Ireland to Russia, but only in the north of Spain and Italy. Resident throughout its range.

Seeing a Grey Partridge has become an event in some parts of the country because its population has diminished so alarmingly. This is the native gamebird of lowland England (unlike the introduced Pheasant and Red-legged Partridge). It is a bird of open grassland where there is the shelter in the form of hedges and copses. Outside the breeding season the Grey Partridge is gregarious, living in tight flocks, flying fast and behaving nervously, either freezing or running away.

In flight it has noisy rapid wing-beats with low glides over the ground. Note the orange edges to the brownish tail

Red-legged Partridge

When flying away the chestnut tail corners contrast with the grey rump and the wings appear plain

The adult is round and stocky with a small head, a white throat patch surrounded by black markings that speckle in the grey breast, a white eyebrow, heavy barring on flanks and red legs

The Red-legged Partridge is naturally restricted to France and Spain. It was introduced into England and Scotland in the 18th century as a sporting quarry, when it was nicknamed the French Partridge, because its red legs were reminiscent of the red gaiters worn by French soldiers. It is slightly larger than its native cousin. It is often seen in flocks and runs away before flying when disturbed.

The ♀ keeps chicks in compact family groups

Golden Plover

FACT FILE

Scientific name
Pluvialis apricaria
Family Plovers
(Charadriidae)
Length 25–28 cm
Wingspan 53–59 cm
Nest Scrape on
ground
Eggs 4, buff,
brown-blotched
Broods 1 per year
Food Insects, worms
Voice Flat, slightly
down-slurred whistle –
'puu'
Size comparison
Slightly smaller than
Lapwing, larger than
Dunlin
Where to see Breeds
on moorland, bogs,
tundra and mountain-
sides above the
treeline in northern
Europe, including
moorland in Britain. In
winter they move
southwards in flocks
to feed on lowland
fields and arable, often
in traditional sites.

*Adults in winter and
juveniles look very
similar with streaked
brown breast merging
into pale belly*

*Adult in
summer has
striking black
breast fringed
with white*

The Golden Plover in breeding plumage is a striking bird. The greenish-yellow back flecked with black gives the golden appearance that in turn gives this plover its name. Even in the winter, when the black breast of the breeding plumage has disappeared, there is a hint of gold to the back and wings. Golden Plovers are mostly seen in winter when they form flocks and are feeding in arable fields often alongside Lapwings and Black-headed Gulls.

*In flight, Golden
Plovers have pointed
wings and fly rapidly
and directly. When in
flocks with Lapwings,
the Golden Plovers are
smaller and do not
have rounded wings*

Grey Plover

In winter adults and juveniles look similar, although the breast of juveniles is more striped. Note the heavy black bill and pale eyebrow

Adult in summer has large extent of black from the face to the belly. Note bulky body and rather hunched posture

FACT FILE

Scientific name
Pluvialis squatoarola

Family Plovers
(Charadriidae)

Length 26-29 cm

Wingspan 56-63 cm

Nest Scrape on
ground

Eggs 4, spotted buff

Broods 1 per year

Food Worms and
other invertebrates

Voice Mournful,
tri-syllabic call

Size comparison
Slightly smaller than
Lapwing, larger than
Dunlin

Where to see Breeds
in the high Arctic
tundra and then moves
south in winter
through Europe,
although some birds
will stop for the winter
in mudflats, sandy and
shingly estuaries.
Wintering birds will
defend feeding
territories against
other Grey Plovers.

In North America the Grey Plover is called the Black-bellied Plover because of its striking and extensive black throat, breast and belly in its breeding plumage, but in most of Europe this tundra-breeding species is seen in its drabber winter plumage. However the black remains in this plumage in dark patches in the 'armpits'. The back is speckled grey (whereas the Golden Plover is speckled yellow).

LOOK-ALIKES

Redshank (p. 140)
Red legs. Longer bill.

**Redshank in flight
(p. 140)** Extensive
white on wings.

Lapwing (pp. 60-61)
Black and white. High
forehead. Crest.

Lapwing in flight
(pp. 60-61) Black and
white. Rounded
wing-tips.

Black-headed Gull in
winter **(pp. 64-65)**
Longer wings.
Distinctly white.

In flight there is a pale wing-bar above the wing and a black patch beneath either wing

137

Snipe

FACT FILE

Scientific name
Gallinago gallinago

Family Sandpipers and their allies (Scolopacidae)

Length 23-28 cm (inc. 7 cm bill)

Wingspan 39-45 cm

Nest Lined scrape on ground

Eggs 4, pale green, brown-blotched

Broods 1 per year

Food Worms, insects and other invertebrates

Voice Harsh call when flushed has been described as being like a rubber boot being withdrawn from mud or a muffled sneeze. It calls from a perch with a sustained 'chip-per chip-per chip-per' with the stress on the first syllable

Size comparison Similar to Moorhen, smaller than Lapwing

Where to see Snipe breed in wet meadows, bogs and marshes across Europe north of the Dordogne and winter in wet places, estuaries, seashore and similar areas to the Mediterranean.

A resting Snipe can have a rather hunched posture. The belly is unmarked. Note the pale crown-stripe and pale eyebrows. Pale streaks along the back are camouflage. Note the very long bill

Once a common bird of wet meadows and fens, the Snipe became scarcer in Britain in the last half of the 20th century. Its diving springtime display was a feature of these places. The bird flies up and then dives steeply with the air vibrating the outer tail feathers to create a drumming sound. When flushed it will often fly away in a zig-zag pattern. The long bill is ideal for probing mud in search of worms and other invertebrates.

When displaying over its territory, the Snipe uses its outer tail feathers to create a drumming sound

Snipe often perch on posts. This individual is standing in upright posture showing that its neck is fairly long

Woodcock

In flight the Woodcock has a 'pot-belly'

FACT FILE

Scientific name
Scolopax rusticola

Family Sandpipers
and their allies
(Scolopacidae)

Length 33-38 cm
(inc. 6-8 cm bill)

Wingspan 55-65 cm

Nest Hollow on round
lined with leaves

Eggs 4, buff,
brown-blotched

Broods 2 per year

Food Worms, insects
and other invertebrates

Voice When ♂ is
roding he gives 3 or 4
grunting notes
followed by a high-
pitched explosive
sound

Size comparison
Larger than Lapwing,
similar to Woodcock

Where to see Breeds
throughout Europe
from Northern Spain in
damp woodlands with
rides, glades or fields.
Eastern and northern
breeding birds move
south-west in winter.
Many of the Woodcock
wintering in England
and Wales have moved
south. On passage and
in winter it may be
found in scrubby and
drier terrain as well as
in woods.

*Adults are very well-camouflaged and
a sitting ♀ is very difficult to see.
Note the steep, angled forehead with
broad pale bars across the head*

The Woodcock is unusual in being a
wading bird that breeds in mixed and
deciduous woodland that has moist enough
soil and leaf-mould in which it can probe
for worms and other invertebrates. Because
it is most active at dawn and dusk, the
Woodcock is most likely to be seen when it
is accidentally flushed during the day or
when the male is performing its territorial
flight at dusk from April to June. This is
known as 'roding' and is a level flight with
rapid wing-beats above the tree tops.

*When roding the wing-
beats are rapid and the
head is held high.
Because of the twilight
conditions, roding birds
are usually seen in
silhouette*

LOOK-ALIKES

Redshank (p. 140)
Reddish-orange legs.
Long legs.

**Common Sandpiper
(p. 145)** Contrast
between pale breast
and dark back. Flicks
tail.

Curlew (pp. 56-57)
Long, down-curved
bill. Long legs.

**Bar-tailed Godwit
(p. 141)** Long, slightly
up-curved bill.

Redshank

In winter the adult has greyer, less streaked plumage and orange-red legs (juveniles have yellow-orange legs)

FACT FILE

Scientific name
Tringa totanus

Family Sandpipers and their allies (Scolopacidae)

Length 24–27 cm

Wingspan 47–53 cm

Nest Hollow on the ground lined with grasses

Eggs 4, buff with blackish blotches

Broods 1 per year

Food Worms, molluscs, crustaceans

Voice The call is a melancholy down-slurred 'te-ew te-ew te-ew'. Its song delivered in flight or from a perch is loud and musical

Size comparison Smaller than Lapwing, larger than Dunlin

Where to see The Redshank is a breeder on inland and coastal marshes, wet meadows and moorland in northern and Eastern Europe. In winter it is seen less commonly inland and usually either found singly or in flocks on or near the coast.

The adult in summer has a pale stripe in front of the eye, a streaked breast, bright orange-red legs, a straight rather stout bill and a finely barred tail

Noisy and common, the Redshank provides a good example for comparison with other waders. Its orange-red legs and orange-based bill are distinctive characteristics (although they are shared by the closely related and rarer Spotted Redshank, which is not included in this book). In flight its combination of white rump and broad white wing-edges is diagnostic.

In flight white rump and broad white wing-edges are noticeable. The toes project beyond the tip of the tail

Bar-tailed Godwit

The adult in summer has a chestnut head, breast and underparts and a black and chestnut spangled back

FACT FILE

Scientific name
Limosa lapponica

Family Sandpipers
and their allies
(Scolopacidae)

Length 33–41 cm

Wingspan 62–72 cm

Nest Hollow on
ground lined with
grasses

Eggs 4, olive,
brown-blotched

Broods 1 per year

Food Molluscs, worms

Voice Sharp 'kirrick
kirrick' call in flight

Size comparison
Larger than Lapwing

Where to see To see
breeding Bar-tailed
Godwits you have to
travel to the tundra of
Lappland or Siberia. In
late summer and early
autumn flocks of these
godwits move
southwards. The
coasts and estuaries of
the British Isles,
France and the
Netherlands provide
rich feeding grounds
for the migrating
birds.

This wader breeds in the open tundra and taiga far in the north of Scandinavia and Russia. It has a short breeding season in the Arctic summer and moves southwards in autumn to winter on the coasts of Western Europe and West Africa. The Bar-tailed Godwit has a slightly uptilted bill.

In flight there is no wing-bar and wings have dark primaries and white rump with barred tailed

LOOK-ALIKES

Snipe (p. 138)
Shortish legs. Long
straight bill.

Curlew in flight
(pp. 56-57) Down-
curved bill. Speckling
on wings.

Oystercatcher in
flight **(p. 146)** Black
and white. Thick
orange-red bill.

Knot

In winter the adult has grey plumage, a pale eyebrow, a rather short black bill and pale green legs

The adult in summer has a chestnut head, breast and underparts with a mottled back

FACT FILE

Scientific name
Calidria canutus

Family Sandpipers and their allies (Scolopacidae)

Length 23-26 cm

Wingspan 47-53 cm

Nest Hollow on ground lined with grasses

Eggs 4, pale green spotted with brown

Broods 1 per year

Food Molluscs, crustaceans, worms

Voice Low 'knut' call

Size comparison Larger than Dunlin, smaller than Lapwing

Where to see This High Arctic breeder is found on tundra in high summer, but is also found on estuaries and sea shores for most of the year. Huge numbers are found in winter on the coastal flats of the British Isles and the rest of western Europe.

This sandpiper's habit of feeding on the water's edge may have led to it being named after King Cnut, who was one of the most famous of English kings even though he wasn't English. For generations, schoolchildren were taught to spell his name only one way – the wrong way. He's best known for sitting on his throne on the seashore and ordering the tide not to come in – although he never believed that the sea would obey him. King Cnut (or Knut, but definitely not Canute, which was a later misspelling to make him sound more English) was probably the most powerful king ever to rule over Anglo-Saxon England.

However, a more probable source may have been an imitation of its call. The Knot is stockier and larger than the other common sandpipers and waders likely to be seen around European coasts. The summer plumage is a striking chestnut, but most of the birds seen around Britain are juveniles or adults in winter, which have grey plumages.

In flight there is a pale grey rump and narrow wing-bars

Sanderling

In winter plumage the adult has black eyes, black bill, black legs, black on bend of wing and grey, almost white, plumage. It makes dashing runs in front of breaking waves

FACT FILE

Scientific name
Calidria alba

Family Sandpipers and their allies (Scolopacidae)

Length 18-21 cm

Wingspan 40-45 cm

Nest Hollow on ground

Eggs 4, greenish with brownish spots

Broods 1 per year

Food Molluscs, crustaceans

Voice Call is a repeated liquid 'quit-quit'

Size comparison Similar to Dunlin

Where to see Breeds on the High Arctic tundra and passes through the North Sea and Atlantic coasts in late summer, autumn and spring on its way to West Africa.

In summer the adult has brown head, throat, upper breast and back with pale underparts

This little wader has really distinctive behaviour when small flocks run rapidly along the tide-edge, stopping and starting in a manner suggestive of mechanical toys. Although it has similar colouring to the Knot in winter, it looks paler because of the striking black legs and bill. When looking at waders on the coast it is relatively easy to identify the little Sanderlings.

In flight the white wing-bar is bold and the dark grey line down the tail has white rump visible on either side

LOOK-ALIKES

Dunlin (pp. 58-59)
Browner. Black, slightly down-curved bill.

Turnstone (p. 144)
Contrast between white underparts and dark back. Pointed bill.

Common Sandpiper (p. 145) Longer body. Contrasting upperparts and underparts. Flicks tail up and down.

Grey Plover (p. 137)
Larger. Longer legs. Plover-like head.

Turnstone

The winter plumage is smudged brown with a boldly marked breast pattern. The legs remain orange

The summer plumage is quite distinctive with orange back with two broad stripes along the back and black-and-white pattern on the face and throat. Note the orange legs and wedge-shaped bill

FACT FILE

Scientific name
Arenaria interpres

Family Sandpipers and their allies (Scolopacidae)

Length 21–24 cm

Wingspan 43–49 cm

Nest Scrape on ground

Eggs 4, greenish brown-blotched

Broods 1 per year

Food Invertebrates

Voice Call is a rattling 'tuk-a-tuk-tuk'

Size comparison Larger than Dunlin

Where to see Breeds in around the rocky, treeless coasts of Scandinavia and winters along the coasts of the British Isles, Western Europe and North Africa.

The distinctive breeding plumage of the Turnstone with its combination of tortoiseshell, black and white is seen in Western Europe, but most of the birds we see are in the rather less dramatic winter plumage. This bird's name accurately describes its feeding habits as it searches for invertebrates beneath stones and among seaweed.

In flight the Turnstone displays more white on the back, wings and tail than any other waders likely to be encountered in Britain except for the Oystercatcher and Avocet

FACT FILE

Scientific name
Actitis hypoleucos

Family Sandpipers
and their allies
(Scolopacidae)

Length 18–20.5 cm

Wingspan 32–35 cm

Nest Hollow on
ground

Eggs 4, buff,
brown-speckled

Broods 1 per year

Food Molluscs,
crustaceans, insects

Voice Rapid series of
clear, falling, whistling
notes is the flight call.
Alarm call is a drawn-
out whistling call.
Song-flight is
twittering and given in
flight low over the
water with pulsating
wings

Size comparison
Similar to Dunlin

Where to see
A summer visitor to
Europe, the Common
Sandpiper breeds near
water, especially with
gravel and shingle
shores, often in
wooded areas. In
Britain it breeds in
upland areas in the
west and north. On
migration single birds
or small groups may
be seen on many types
of water body.

The Common Sandpiper has a long-bodied appearance with a long tail and rather short legs. There is a noticeable white gap between the wings and dark breast

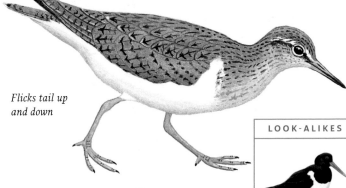

Flicks tail up and down

This is one of the most widely distributed common waders, which depending on the time of year can be seen in a great variety of wetland habitats, especially when migrating. Its short legs and habit of flicking its rather long tail up and down, are distinctive characteristics of this rather smart wader.

In flight there are conspicuous wing-bars

LOOK-ALIKES

**Oystercatcher
(p. 146)** Larger. Black
and white. Orange-red
bill.

Knot (p. 142) Grey.
Black bill. Slightly
larger.

Sanderling in autumn
plumage **(p. 143)**
Smaller. Grey back.
Black bill.

Dunlin in summer
plumage **(p. 58–59)**
Rusty brown back.
Black belly. Down-
curved bill.

Oystercatcher

In winter there is a white collar and the tip of the bill becomes dark

FACT FILE

Scientific name
Haematopus ostralegus
Family Oystercatchers (Haematopidae)
Length 39–44 cm
Wingspan 72–83 cm
Nest Scrape in shingle and sand
Eggs 3, black-blotched buff
Broods 1 per year
Food Molluscs, worms, crustaceans
Voice Loud, far-carrying 'kleep'. Bubbling song is given by both sexes in flight often together
Size comparison Larger than Lapwing, smaller than Curlew
Where to see Oystercatchers breed around coasts. They winter in flocks around the coasts from southern Scandinavia southwards. Some breed in broad, shingly river valleys and at gravel pits.

The adult in summer is black and white apart from a long orange-red bill, pink legs and orange-red eyes

The black-and-white plumage and the long red bill of the Oystercatcher makes it very difficult to mistake for any other species. It is the most noticeable wader around the coast throughout the year. The hefty bill is used to prise shellfish from rocks and for breaking into the shells of bivalves such as cockles.

In flight the wings have broad wing-bars are white and there is extensive white on the rump

Avocet

To find its food of small crustaceans and aquatic insects, the Avocet sweeps the surface with its bill

The adult has a thin, uptilted bill and long pale blue legs. It is about the same size as an Oystercatcher, but more slender and with noticeably longer legs

FACT FILE

Scientific name
Recurvirostra avosetta

Family Avocets and Stilts (Recurvirostridae)

Length 42–46 cm

Wingspan 67–77 cm

Nest Scrape on island

Eggs 4, buff, spotted and blotched with black

Broods 1 per year

Food Insects, crustaceans

Voice The loud piping 'kloo-ep, kloo-ep, kloo-ep' has a ringing tone

Size comparison Slightly smaller Curlew, larger than Black-headed Gull

Where to see Breeds in isolated colonies on flat, open shores, shallow brackish lagoons and sandy shoals. In winter it is found in mudflats and estuaries with some migrating to the Mediterranean and African coasts.

The Avocet in Britain represents a success story for the RSPB's conservation management. After an absence of more than a century and a half this species was found in the 1940s to be breeding at two sites in Suffolk. Now Avocets breed on coastal marshes from Lincolnshire to Hampshire and wintering flocks may be seen on estuaries along the south coast of England. No other European species has such an up-curved bill.

In flight, the white on the wings contrasts with the black head, wing-tips and patches on the wings

LOOK-ALIKES

Lapwing (pp. 60–61)
Smaller. Green-black back and wings. Tuft on head. Short bill.

Turnstone (p. 144)
Short orange legs. Short bill. Mottled back.

Curlew (pp. 56–57)
Larger. Bill curved down.

Black-headed Gull (pp. 64–65)
Chocolate-brown head. Short red-billed. Grey back.

Ringed Plover

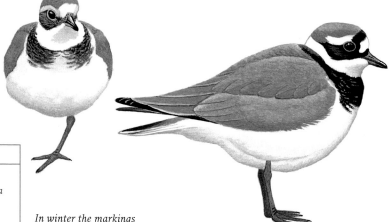

FACT FILE

Scientific name
Charadrius hiaticula

Family Plovers
(Charadriidae)

Length 17–19.5 cm

Wingspan 35–41 cm

Nest Scrape on the
ground

Eggs 4,
brown-spotted, buff

Broods 2–3 per year

Food Insects,
crustaceans, molluscs

Voice Soft two-
syllable call stressing
the first syllable and
rising on the second.
Song a mellow
variation of this

Size comparison
Similar to Dunlin

Where to see Breeds
on shingle on open
coasts, gravel pits and
rivers in N. Europe,
wintering in British
Isles, North Sea coast,
Mediterranean and
further south.

*In winter the markings
are fainter and the bill
dark brown, but the legs
remain orange*

*The adult in summer has black
markings on the upper breast,
black and white facial markings,
orange legs and a short, thick
orange bill with a black tip. Note
that the wing-tips reach almost
to the tip of the tail when at rest*

The Ringed Plover and the Little Ringed Plover look very similar,
which is not usually an identification problem because they tend
to occupy different habitats, but they overlap in England, where
both now breed in gravel pits where there are open shingle banks.
The Ringed Plover is more widespread in Northern Europe and is
a common seashore bird in Britain and Ireland. Like other plovers,
the female will distract predators from her young by pretending to
have an injured wing.

*The pale wing-bars
show up well in flight*

Little Ringed Plover

Adult in summer has a more slender appearance than the Ringed Plover because it has longer, more slender legs, a longer, darker bill and a more slender rump and tail.

Note the yellow ring around the eye and the pale narrow band on the head. Note that the tail extends beyond the wing-tips at rest

Adult in winter has a less well-defined plumage pattern with the cheek marking coming to a point rather than being rounded (as in the Ringed Plover)

It was in the 1940s that the Little Ringed Plover was first discovered to be breeding in southern England on gravel pits, a habitat that was increasing as more gravel was needed to rebuild the post-war infrastructure. As the pits become more vegetated the Little Ringed Plover moved to more open pits elsewhere. Elsewhere in Europe it may breed on shingle expanses of large rivers.

In flight the wing-bar is so fine that it might be invisible and the white collar is very narrow

LOOK-ALIKES

Turnstone in winter **(p. 144)** More hunched. Mottled back. Wedge-shaped bill. Very little white on face.

Lapwing (pp. 60–61) Taller. Crest. Orange under tail.

Dunlin in summer plumage **(pp. 58–59)** Longer. Black down-curved bill. Black belly.

Dunlin in winter **(pp. 58–59)** Longer. Black down-curved bill. No black plumage.

Puffin

In winter the bill becomes smaller and face greyer

In summer the adult has a white face, a red, yellow and blue bill with orange legs and feet

FACT FILE

Scientific name
Fratercula artica

Family Auks (Alcidae)

Length 28–34 cm

Wingspan 50–60 cm

Nest Burrow on steep, grassy sea cliffs

Eggs 1, white

Broods 1 per year

Food Fish, crustaceans, molluscs

Voice The call, usually made in its burrow, is a deep, grunting 'arr-uh'

Size comparison
Slightly smaller than Guillemot

Where to see Puffins breed in colonies on slopes above coastal cliffs in Britain (largely in the west and north), Brittany, Ireland, Iceland and Norway. They arrive at their breeding colonies in March and have left by early August to spend the winter at sea in the Atlantic.

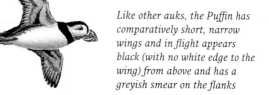

Like other auks, the Puffin has comparatively short, narrow wings and in flight appears black (with no white edge to the wing) from above and has a greyish smear on the flanks

At close range the Puffin is unmistakable because of its rather rounded clownish appearance. In flight it may be confused with the other common auks, the Guillemot and the Razorbill, both of which are larger and look longer. Although the Puffin is numerous it is restricted to relative few colonies on the sea cliffs on either side of the Atlantic. When fishing it dives from the surface and uses its wings to fly underwater in pursuit of small fish.

At breeding colonies good views of Puffins can be obtained as they return to burrows with food for the young

Razorbill

The adult has a black head, back and wings and a short deep bill with a narrow downward white stripe on either side

In winter the chin and part of the head become white

FACT FILE

Scientific name
Alca torda

Family Auks (Alcidae)

Length 38-43 cm

Wingspan 60-69 cm

Nest Crevice among boulders

Eggs 1, variably blotched brown

Broods 1 per year

Food Fish, crustaceans, molluscs

Voice Rarely utters, but breeding birds may give very deep creaking growls and grunts

Size comparison Similar to Guillemot

Where to see Many Razorbills return between late February and April to their breeding areas on sea-cliffs. By August many have moved from breeding areas to the north Atlantic, but increasing numbers return early to their breeding areas.

This is the quietest of the auks that commonly breed in northern Europe. They are found with colonies of other species of auks and gulls, but the razorbills tend to be discrete from each other, nesting among boulder scree, often below the noisy Guillemots closely packed on cliff-ledges. Its neck looks rather thicker than the Guillemot's.

In flight the Razorbill looks black from above with white clearly visible on either side of the rump. The underwing area is white (compare with the Guillemot's smudgy 'armpit')

LOOK-ALIKES

Guillemot in flight **(pp. 62-63)** Looks chocolate-brown in flight. Pointed bill.

Guillemot (pp. 62-63) Brown back and wings. Pointed bill.

Lesser Black-backed Gull (p. 156) Longer wings with white edges. White head.

Oystercatcher in flight **(p. 146)** More extensive white plumage. Bright orange-red bill.

Fulmar

The Fulmar on its nest looks rather bulky. The bill which has a hooked tip looks thick because of the tube nostrils

In flight the wings are held stiffly. There are several colour variations: this is a dark phase, a variation that is most common among the most northerly populations

FACT FILE

Scientific name
Fulmarus glacialis

Family Petrels and Fulmars (Procellaridae)

Length 43–52 cm

Wingspan 101–117 cm

Nest On ledges and in burrows

Eggs 1, white

Broods 1 per year

Food Crustaceans, fish and fish offal

Voice Throaty, cackling calls mostly at breeding colonies

Size comparison Similar to Guillemot

Where to see Breeds on ledges, in burrows and on buildings on coastal cliffs, spending the rest of the year in the North Atlantic and North Sea.

Until the beginning of the 20th century, the Fulmar was confined as a breeding bird to the cliffs of Iceland, Faeroe and Norway, but the population increased rapidly and it now breeds on suitable coastal cliffs to as far south as Brittany. Despite its superficial similarity to a gull, its shape is quite distinctive. The narrow wings with parallel edges are held stiffly as it soars on rising air currents, rarely flapping its wings. The high, rounded forehead with a hooked tip and tube nostrils and the thick neck give it a very different expression from any gull's.

When swimming, its neck looks thicker than a gull's and the bill is noticeably thick. It is a long-lived species, some individuals surviving for over 50 years.

Kittiwake

In flight the summer adult shows grey wings with very black tips, as if they had been dipped in black ink

The adult has rather short black legs, a greenish yellow, pointed bill, a notched tail and a rather 'sweet' expression

FACT FILE

Scientific name *Rissa tridactyla*

Family Gulls and Terns (Laridae)

Length 37–42 cm

Wingspan 62–69 cm

Nest Cup of seaweed on cliff-ledges

Eggs 2, brown, speckled, creamy

Broods 1 per year

Food Fish, crustaceans, fish offal

Voice Call is a quick, nasal, repeated 'kitti-waake' with the emphasis on the second syllable

Size comparison Similar to Black-headed Gull, smaller than Guillemot

Where to see This colonially breeding gull spends much of its year at sea, coming ashore to breed on steep cliffs south from northern Scandinavia to Brittany, with two isolated colonies in Portugal.

This gull, which is slightly larger than the Black-headed Gull, is rarely seen far from the sea. Its quick, stiff wing-beats are rather tern-like, but its wing-tips are black. The wings are a soft dove-grey in breeding plumage. It breeds in colonies, some containing many thousands of pairs.

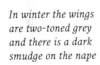

In winter the wings are two-toned grey and there is a dark smudge on the nape

The juvenile (known as a 'tarrock') has well-marked dark V-markings on the wings and there is a black crescent on the tip of the tail

LOOK-ALIKES

Herring Gull (p. 155) Large. White patch on black wing-tip.

Common Gull (p. 154) White patch on black wing-tip.

Black-headed Gull in winter **(pp. 64–65)** Broad white leading edge to forewing. Wings less pointed.

Common Gull

FACT FILE

Scientific name
Larus canus

Family Gulls and
Terns (Laridae)

Length 40–46 cm

Wingspan 99–108 cm

Nest Lined hollow on
ground

Eggs 3, pale green,
brown-blotched

Broods 1 per year

Food Invertebrates

Voice Laughing
'kee-ah' call that is
higher pitched than
the Herring Gull's

Size comparison Very
slightly larger than
Black-headed Gull

Where to see Breeds
colonially and
sometimes singly
along coasts, in
marshes, along rivers
and on inland water
eastwards from Ireland
to Scandinavia and
into Asia. Nests on
boulders and other
elevated positions.
Britain and Ireland are
the main wintering
areas with isolated
wintering grounds in
the eastern
Mediterranean and
further south.

*In flight there is a
large white area
at the wing-tips*

*The adult in summer has a
greenish-yellow pointed bill, a dark
eye and yellowish green legs with a
broad white band between the grey
of the wings and black wing-tips*

Despite its name, this is not the commonest European gull,
although it is very numerous in winter in Britain and Ireland. In
North America it is known as the Mew Gull ('mew' is an old
English name for a gull). It is often seen in winter in flocks with
Black-headed Gulls resting or feeding on playing fields and other
grasslands.

*The adult in winter
has faint grey
streaks on the head*

*The immature is less
heavily streaked than the
immature Herring Gull*

Herring Gull

The juvenile are mottled with pale patches on the tips of the tertials

The adult has a pale eye, a stout yellow bill with a red circle, pink legs and large white spots on the wing-tips when folded

One of the most familiar gulls, the Herring Gull is the archetypal 'sea-gull', although it is frequently seen inland in flocks on open fields, reservoirs and lakes. There are considerable differences in the plumages of large gulls of different ages and the full adult plumage is not apparent until after the second winter.

In flight, the juvenile (left) shows a pale patch on the wings and there is only a moderate contrast between the rump and the tail band (see Lesser Black-backed Gull)

LOOK-ALIKES

Kittiwake (p. 153) Daintier. Uniformly grey wings. Inky black wing-tips.

Fulmar (p. 152) Straight narrow wings. Rounded head. Tubenose.

Black-headed Gull in winter (pp. 64–65) Smaller. Pointed wings. White fore edge to wing.

Lesser Black-backed Gull (p. 156) Darker back.

Lesser Black-backed Gull immature (p. 156) Darker wing tips. Contrast between rump and tail band.

Lesser Black-backed Gull

The juvenile is mottled grey-brown (and similar to juvenile Herring Gull) and the tips of the areas around the eyes are often dark

FACT FILE

Scientific name
Larus fuscus

Family Gulls and Terns (Laridae)

Length 48–56 cm

Wingspan 117–134 cm

Nest Lined hollow on ground

Eggs 3, dark-blotched, olive

Broods 1 per year

Food Omnivorous

Voice Similar call to Herring Gull, but deeper and more nasal

Size comparison Larger than Black-headed Gull

Where to see Breeds along coasts and around lakes in northern Europe. Those breeding in Scandinavia and Russia winter in the Middle East and Africa, migrating across Europe along river valleys, while Western European breeders move less far and many winter in Britain and Ireland, moving inland to fields, landfill sites and inland waters.

The adult in summer has a dark slate-grey back and wings, a yellow bill with red spot and yellow legs

The race breeding around the Baltic is very dark slate-grey and may be seen in Britain in winter

This gull is of a similar size to the Herring Gull and looks similar with the exception of the darker back and wings. There are similarities with the Great Black-backed Gull, which is larger, bulkier and fiercer-looking than the Lesser Black-backed Gull. Lesser Black-backed are seen inland.

In flight the immature has no pale patches on the wings...

second winter has a dark back with some mottling still visible...

the adult has a broken wing edge to the tips of the trailing edges of the wings

Great Black-backed Gull

The juvenile has mottled plumage with greater contrast than the Lesser Black-backed Gull. Note heavy black bill

FACT FILE

Scientific name
Larus marinus

Family Gulls and Terns (Laridae)

Length 61–74 cm

Wingspan 144–166 cm

Nest Pile of sticks and seaweed on ground

Eggs 2–3, brown speckled, olive brown

Broods 1 per year

Food Seabirds, offal, carrion

Voice Much deeper, hoarse, gruff version of Herring Gull and Lesser Black-backed Gull's call

Size comparison Smaller than Cormorant, much larger than Black-headed Gull

Where to see Breeds around the coasts of Iceland and Ireland, Scotland, Wales, south-west England and Scandinavia and winters in the North Sea and Western Approaches. Usually seen on the coast, but increasingly seen inland in Britain.

The Great Black-backed Gull is much bulkier than the Lesser Black-backed Gull. It has a noticeable thick yellow bill with a red spot, large white marks on the folded wings and dusky pink legs

This is a gull that really deserves the description 'great', because it is almost as large as a Greylag Goose. It is a fierce predator attacking adult as well as juvenile birds and a pirate that steals food from other birds such as cormorants, sea ducks and herons. It has a much larger bill than other gulls.

In flight, the adult has broad wings with a broad white margin all the way along the trailing edge of the wings and with a white patch towards the wing-tip

In flight the juvenile's wings are dark towards the tips and paler nearer the body

LOOK-ALIKES

Herring Gull (p. 155) Grey back. Pink legs.

Herring Gull immature **(p. 155)** Mottled edges to tertial wing feathers.

Fulmar (p. 152) Straight, narrow wings. Tubenose.

Guillemot (pp. 62–63) Extensive dark plumage. Pointed bill. Upright stance.

Arctic Tern

FACT FILE

Scientific name
Sterna paradisaea

Family Gulls and
Terns (Laridae)

Length 33-39 cm
(inc. 7-11.5 cm tail
streamers)

Wingspan 70-80 cm

Nest Scrape on ground

Eggs 2, buff,
brown-blotched

Broods 1 per year

Food Fish

Voice Piping, clear
repeated 'kee-er' notes
similar to Common
Tern, but more abrupt

Size comparison
Similar to Common
Tern

Where to see
Summer visitor to
Europe from late April
to October, which
breeds usually in
colonies around coasts
on islands, marshes,
dunes, tundra and
barren mountainsides.
Winters in southern
Africa.

*Juvenile (above) has more black
on head than Common Tern and
usually less brown on the back*

*The adult in summer has a dark red
bill (with no black tip), very short
red legs, long tail-streamers and a
greyish breast contrasting with
distinct white cheek*

The long tail streamers of the Arctic Tern make the vernacular
name of 'sea swallow' very appropriate. It is so similar to the
Common Tern (see pp. 66-67) that when birdwatchers do not
have a good enough view to see the diagnostic characters clearly
they will describe the unidentified bird as a 'comic tern'. However,
with good views it is usually possible to sort the two species out.
Arctic Terns are rarely seen inland. The Arctic Tern migrates to
South Africa in autumn, making one of the champion
long-distance migrants.

*In flight the underside of
the wing-tip has a narrow,
distinct, dark mark*

Sandwich Tern

The juvenile has a short tail (wings are longer when folded), black legs and a barred grey back

FACT FILE

Scientific name
Sterna sandvicensis

Family Gulls and Terns (Laridae)

Length 37-43 cm

Wingspan 85-97 cm

Nest Scrape on ground

Eggs 1-2, buff, brown-speckled

Broods 1 per year

Food Fish

Voice Loud 'kerrick' with stress on final syllable (has been described as sounding like amalgam being pressed into a tooth!). Very noisy at breeding colonies

Size comparison Larger than Common Tern, similar to Black-headed Gull

Where to see Summer visitor to northern Europe from late March to late September, breeding in colonies on sandy beaches, low islands in salt or brackish water. It winters in southern Europe and North Africa. It is rarely seen inland.

The adult in summer has a black cap with shaggy crest, a black bill with pale yellow tip, black legs and wings that reach the end of the tail when folded

The shaggy crest of the Sandwich Tern makes it very different from the other British species of terns. It is larger and when feeding will plunge from a greater height than Common or Arctic Terns. It breeds in colonies on low-lying coasts.

In flight there is a short forked tail, a darkish wedge to wing tip with a weak dark mark on underside (from June/July a white forehead develops and crest becomes less shaggy)

LOOK-ALIKES

Common Tern in summer **(pp. 66-67)** Black tip to bill. Long head. More white on breast. Longer legs.

Common Tern in flight, summer **(pp. 66-67)** Translucent inner primaries. Indistinct dark mark on underside of wing tip.

Common Tern in winter **(pp. 66-67)** Bill looks shorter than Arctic Tern.

Black-headed Gull in summer **(pp. 64-65)** Dark brown head. Larger.

Coot

The juvenile (left) has a pale throat and cheeks but no white on the body. Note the frilly feet

FACT FILE

Scientific name
Fulica atra

Family Rails and Crakes (Rallidae)

Length 36-42 cm

Wingspan 70-80 cm

Nest Cup of vegetation among vegetation at water's edge

Eggs 6-9, black-spotted buff

Broods 2 per year

Food Omnivorous, but mainly plants

Voice Varied calls include loud hoarse 'kook'

Size comparison Larger than Moorhen, smaller than Mallard

Where to see Widely distributed across Europe. Eastern breeding birds move west in winter and large flocks build in harbours and inland waters in Western Europe. Favoured habitat is larger water bodies and broad, slow-flowing rivers.

In short flight, the coot trails its legs

In the water, the Coot has a more rounded appearance than the Moorhen (see pp. 68–69) and nods its head less jerkily. Note the white bill and facial shield extending from it

This plump bird is a common and noisy waterbird found throughout Britain except the far north of Scotland. It feeds on a variety of food, much of which it finds by diving underwater. In winter, Coots are seen in large flocks. In spring and early summer they vigorously defend their territories.

The chick is fluffy and red-headed

Rivals fight with their feet and balance with their wings amid enormous splashing

Little Grebe

In winter the throat becomes pale. Note the rounded head and short bill

FACT FILE

Scientific name
Tachybaptus ruficollis

Family Grebes
(Podicipitidae)

Length 23-29 cm

Wingspan 40-45 cm

Nest Floating mound
of vegetation anchored
to emerging plants

Eggs 4-6, white

Broods 2 per year

Food Fish, aquatic
insects, crustaceans
and molluscs

Voice High-pitched
rattling trill during the
breeding season,
sounding rather like ♂
Cuckoo. Silent outside
the breeding season

Size comparison
Smaller than Moorhen

Where to see Breeds
eastwards across
Europe from Ireland
into Russia and as far
north as southern
Sweden. Mainly
resident in the west
with eastern breeders
moving westwards in
autumn. Needs rivers
and waterbodies with
well-vegetated banks.

*The adult in summer has a chestnut
throat and neck with noticeable
yellow skin around the bill*

*The chick has a
striped head and
pinkish bill*

The Little Grebe, which is smaller than any
other British waterbird, sometimes seems
to sit on the water in the bouncy manner of
a plastic duck, especially when its plumage
is fluffed up. It dives in search of food and
will emerge many metres away. During the
breeding season, despite its rather smart
plumage, the Little Grebe is unobtrusive,
which means it is
more likely to be
seen in winter.

*The nest is a
floating mass of
vegetation*

LOOK-ALIKES

Moorhen (pp. 68-69)
Upright tail, swims
with nodding head.

**Great Crested Grebe
(pp. 72-73)** Long
neck, pointed bill,
feather-fringed face.

**Tufted Duck ♀
(p. 166)** Duck-shaped
bill, very rounded head.

Pochard ♀ (p. 167)
Duck-shaped bill, very
rounded head.

Shoveler

♂ has a green head with yellow eye, a white breast and chestnut sides and underparts

♀ is mottled, and looks very like a female mallard with a very large bill

In late summer, ♂ moults into eclipse and looks similar to ♀ but with a darker head

FACT FILE

Scientific name
Anas clypeata

Family Ducks and Geese (Anatidae)

Length 44–52 cm

Wingspan 73–82 cm

Nest Hollow in grass near water

Eggs 8–12, buff

Broods 1 per year

Food Seeds, plant material, molluscs, crustaceans

Voice ♂ call is a harsh 'took, took' while the ♀ quacks

Size comparison Smaller than Mallard, similar to Great Crested Grebe

Where to see Breeds along the shores of shallow lakes and in marshes with open water across Europe. Moves southwards in winter to Western Europe and the Mediterranean. Usually seen around the margins of lakes in winter in small flocks or individuals.

The large flat bill of the Shoveler contains a complex arrangement of filters which catch the floating material as it sieves water. It feeds by sweeping its bill across the surface of the water. This is a surface-feeding duck that rides low in the water with a rather front-heavy appearance. It chooses the shallower parts of lakes in which to find food. Shovelers tend to be migratory.

In flight, ♂ shows pale blue forewing

In flight, ♀ shows grey forewing. Note the stumpy rear end and contrasting heavy head and long bill

To feed, the Shoveler sweeps its bill across the water just beneath the surface

Shelduck

In flight, white forewing contrasts with the rest of the wing being dark

♂ has a dark bottle green head, a broad chestnut band around the breast and a red bill with pronounced basal knob

♀ has a dark bottle green head, a broad chestnut band around the breast and a red bill with no knob

FACT FILE

Scientific name
Tadorna tadorna

Family Ducks and Geese (Anatidae)

Length 55-65 cm

Wingspan 100-120 cm

Nest Cup lined with down in burrow or hollow tree

Eggs 8-15 cream

Broods 1 per year

Food Crustaceans, molluscs

Voice ♂ has a high whistling call as it pursues a ♀ in flight. ♀ emits a nasal whinnying

Size comparison Slightly larger than Mallard, smaller than Cormorant

Where to see This is mainly a coastal duck breeding around Europe. Some may be found along larger rivers and on lakes. It may breed some distance from water and move its young to the coast after they have hatched. In late summer large numbers gather at a few estuaries and mudflats.

There is a somewhat goose-like appearance to this duck. It stands upright and has a waddling gait. With good views it is possible to differentiate between males and females. From a distance, the Shelduck may appear to be black and white. On mudflats in summer large numbers of young Shelducks can be seen with adults.

Feeds by taking molluscs from the surface of the mud

LOOK-ALIKES

Mallard ♂ (pp. 70-71) Metallic green head. Yellow bill. No white on body.

Teal ♂ (p. 164) Small, perky shape.

Mallard ♀ (pp. 70-71) Less regularly mottled, smaller bill than Shoveler.

Wigeon ♂ (p. 165) Brown head with yellow forehead. Small slightly upturned bill.

Teal

♀ is neatly streaked and speckled. On each wing there is a bright green patch called a 'speculum'

FACT FILE

Scientific name
Anas crecca

Family Ducks and Geese (Anatidae)

Length 34–38 cm

Wingspan 53–59 cm

Nest Lined hollow in march plants

Eggs 8–12, creamy buff

Broods 1 per year

Food Seeds, aquatic plants

Voice ♂ has high-pitched, clear whistle and ♀ quacks

Size comparison Smaller than Mallard, slightly larger than Moorhen

Where to see Most Teal in Europe breed north from northern France with the most northerly and easterly populations moving south in winter. It breeds on fresh and brackish lakes and ponds and on well-vegetated seashores.

♂ is largely grey with spotted buff breast, a creamy yellow triangle at rear and a white horizontal stripe

This is the smallest duck found in Britain and Ireland, being only slightly larger than a Moorhen. The delicate patterning of the male's head and the creamy yellow triangle beneath the tail is only easily seen when the birds are close (as from a hide on a nature reserve). When flushed, Teals will spring into the air almost vertically.

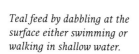

Teal feed by dabbling at the surface either swimming or walking in shallow water. This is a ♂ in eclipse

In flight the wings are narrow and pointed with short neck and fast wing-beats. Note the green specula on the wings

Wigeon

♂ has a reddish head with yellow front, a pale pink breast and a grey body with white and black rear end

♀ is cinnamon above and below with pale speckled rear end

FACT FILE

Scientific name
Anas penelope

Family Ducks and Geese (Anatidae)

Length 42–50 cm

Wingspan 71–85 cm

Nest Lined hollow

Eggs 7–8, creamy

Broods 1 per year

Food Plants and seeds

Voice ♂ has loud, long whistle. ♀ gives a subdued growl

Size comparison
Slightly smaller than Mallard

Where to see Breeds in the north of Europe from the Scottish Highlands to Iceland and Scandinavia on forest lakes, tundra pools and marshes. It winters around European coasts and on inland lakes in flocks.

In winter Wigeon are often seen grazing in flocks near water

The high, rounded forehead and pale blue bill gives the Wigeon a rather sweet appearance. The creamy-yellow front of the head contrasts with male's reddish head and neck. The female is less speckled than other female ducks. The tail comes to a slender point.

In flight, ♂ has very noticeable white wing patches. Both sexes have white breasts. The head is prominent and there is a pointed tail

LOOK-ALIKES

Mallard ♂ (pp. 70-71) Longer neck. Plain green head.

Mallard ♀ (pp. 70-71) Longer neck. Blue speculum.

Pochard ♀ (p. 167) Larger. Dished bill. Dives low in water.

Moorhen (pp. 68-69) Large body. Small head.

Little Grebe (p. 161) Small. Dumpy.

Tufted Duck

♂ in eclipse is more boldly marked than ♀

FACT FILE

Scientific name
Aythya fulica

Family Ducks and Geese (Anatidae)

Length 40-47 cm

Wingspan 65-72 cm

Nest Well-hidden lined hollow

Eggs 5-12, greenish

Broods 1 per year

Food Aquatic plants and invertebrates

Voice Rather silent, but ♂ has bubbly series of notes that accelerate. ♀ growls

Size comparison Smaller than Mallard, larger than Moorhen

Where to see Breeds in a wide variety of wetland habitats from tundra pools to lakes in municipal parks from France to Iceland. Most populations are migratory, moving south and west in autumn. Large numbers winter in the British isles and elsewhere in Western Europe.

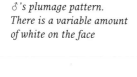

♂ in breeding plumage has long tuft

♀ is brown with paler flanks echoing ♂'s plumage pattern. There is a variable amount of white on the face

Both sexes show wide white wing-bars in flight. Note pointed wings and fast wing-beats

The rounded shape with the large rounded head and rather thin neck is distinctive. The male's long tuft is very obvious, but a tuft is visible on most females. Outside the breeding season the often dense flocks of Tufted Ducks contain both males and females.

♀ with chocolate-brown ducklings

♂ diving from the surface

Pochard

♀ has a grey-brown back and flanks, a dark brown breast, a brown face with pale eye-ring and line from eye and a grey band on the bill (juvenile birds are similar to ♀ but browner)

♂ has a reddish brown head, a black breast, a black rear, pale grey back and flanks and a grey band on bill

FACT FILE

Scientific name
Aythya ferina

Family Ducks and Geese (Anatidae)

Length 42-49 cm

Wingspan 67-75 cm

Nest Mound of vegetation near water's edge

Eggs 6-11, greenish

Broods 1 per year

Food Aquatic plants and invertebrates

Voice Tends to be silent outside the breeding season when ♂ has a wheezing growl and ♀ has loud purr

Size comparison
Slightly smaller than Mallard, similar to Great Crested Grebe

Where to see Breeds near lakes and marshes where there is water over 1 m deep, across Europe with the northern and eastern populations moving west and south in winter.

This is a common diving duck on reservoirs and gravel-pits in winter, when the flocks tend to be largely composed of males, which are more gregarious than females. There is an indeterminate quality to the females which may provide an identification when they are seen on their own. The outline of the head is characteristic with the sloping forehead and longish bill. Pochards usually dive for food, but they may also up-end like dabbling ducks.

When taking off, Pochards often run across the surface

In flight, the body looks heavy, with rapid wing-beats. There is broad greyish wing-bar fringed with black on the trailing edge

LOOK-ALIKES

Coot (p. 160)
Rounded, black body. White bill.

Shoveler (p. 162)
Long body. Large bill and head.

Mallard ♀ (pp. 70-71)
Larger. Speckled plumage. Longer neck.

Mallard ♂ (p. 70)
Green head. Longish neck.

Shag

Juvenile's breast is uniformly brownish and the feet are pale

In breeding plumage the adult has glossy dark green plumage and a yellow gape

In winter, the adult has very dark green plumage, a dark face, a pronounced forehead and a narrow, dark bill

FACT FILE

Scientific name
Phalacrocorax aristotelis

Family Cormorants and Shags (Phalacrocoracidae)

Length 68-78 cm

Wingspan 95-110 cm

Nest Mound of seaweed

Eggs 3, pale

Broods 1 per year

Food Fish

Voice Clicks and grunts at breeding sites, but usually silent outside the breeding season

Size comparison Smaller than Cormorant

Where to see This coastal bird breeds around the coasts of Europe including the Mediterranean. It is mainly resident.

In flight, the wings are rather rounded and shorter than Cormorant's. The neck is straight and narrow

In breeding plumage the Shag has glossy dark green plumage and a crest. When light catches the back, it has a metallic sheen. Outside the breeding season there is a similarity with the Cormorant (see p. 76), but the Shag is slightly smaller and thinner. The forehead of the Shag is more pronounced than the Cormorant's.

On the water, the body of the Shag is shorter than that of the Cormorant and, when diving, there is a pronounced leap out of the water

Gannet

The adult in summer has a lemon yellow head (which becomes paler in winter) and black feet with pale blue stripes along the toes

The juvenile has dark mottled plumage, sometimes seeming almost black

FACT FILE

Scientific name
Morus bassanus

Family Gannets and Boobies (Sulidae)

Length 85-97 cm

Wingspan 170-192 cm

Nest Mound of seaweed

Eggs 1, white

Broods 1 per year

Food Fish

Voice Grunts and grating cackles at breeding colonies

Size comparison Similar to Cormorant

Where to see Breeds in colonies on steep rocky coasts of Iceland, Norway, Britain, Ireland, Brittany and the Channel Islands. Outside the breeding season Gannets are found in North Sea, North Atlantic and the western Mediterranean. Rarely seen inland unless driven in by storms.

A greater amount of white shows in the plumage as the bird becomes older. This bird immediately to the right is in its third autumn

In flight the wings are long with black tips. The body is cigar-shaped. Looks very white

The great majority of the world's Gannets breed on the coasts of Western Europe. The size and the whiteness of the adults are unlike any of the species found in these waters. It takes more than three years for Gannets to achieve their adult plumage, but dark immature birds can be identified by their cigar-shaped bodies and long wings.

Gannets fish by diving from a height of usually about 9 m to grasp the fish in their bill

LOOK-ALIKES

Cormorant in flight (pp. 76-77) Thick, kinked neck. More pointed wings. White flank patch in breeding plumage.

Cormorant in winter (pp. 76-77) Thick neck. Thicker bill.

Great Crested Grebe in winter (pp. 72-73) Pointed bill. Slender neck.

Great Crested Grebe in flight (pp. 72-73) Humped back. Narrow neck. Feet sticking out. Short wings.

Brent Goose

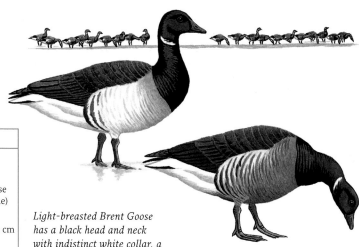

FACT FILE

Scientific name
Branta bernicla

Family Ducks, Geese and Swans (Anatidae)

Length 55–62 cm

Wingspan 120–142 cm

Nest Lined scrape near water

Eggs 3–5, yellowish white

Broods 1 per year

Food Eel-grass, grass, cereals, marsh plants

Voice Guttural 'grook' call, making a grumbling sound in flocks

Size comparison Similar to Mallard

Where to see This tundra-breeding goose moves south in late autumn and winters on the coasts of western Europe, returning to their breeding grounds in May. It feeds on eel-grass and other maritime plants and grazes on coastal marshes and meadows.

Light-breasted Brent Goose has a black head and neck with indistinct white collar, a dark grey faintly barred back, a pale grey belly and an extensive white under tail

Dark-breasted Brent Goose has a black head and neck with indistinct white collar, a dark grey back, a dark grey belly and extensive white under tail

This is a small goose, which behaves in many ways like a duck. There are two races. The 'pale-breasted' breeds in Greenland and Canada and winters in Ireland with another population from Spitsbergen and Franz Joseph Land, island groups north of Norway, wintering in Denmark and Northumberland. The 'dark-breasted' race breeds in Arctic Russia and winters on the North Sea and English Channel coasts.

In flight a V-shaped white mark on tail and broad black trailing edge are clear

The adult has a thick neck, a large head with face that looks pale against its dark neck, a heavy orange bill and dull pink legs

FACT FILE

Scientific name
Anser anser

Family Ducks, Geese and Swans (Anatidae)

Length 74-84 cm

Wingspan 149-168 cm

Nest Scrape near water

Eggs 4-6, white

Broods 1 per year

Food Grass, grain, roots

Voice Highly vocal with deep, raw 'aahng, ung, ung' call

Size comparison Smaller than Canada Goose, larger than Mallard

Where to see Breeds in the British Isles, Iceland, Scandinavia and Eastern Europe near shallow lakes, reedbeds, freshwater marshes, rocky coasts and coastal islets. This is the only grey goose to be seen in summer in Europe in large numbers in summer. Most populations are migratory, wintering in countries bordering the North Sea and in the Mediterranean and Baltic Seas.

In flight, the leading edges of the wings are very pale grey contrasting with dark trailing edge

This is the archetypal grey goose and the one from which domestic geese were first bred. Wild Greylags are migratory, but much of the British population (descended from feral birds released in the last century) stays throughout the year forming flocks in winter and grazing on pasture, stubble and playing fields.

The goslings are pale yellow

LOOK-ALIKES

Canada Goose in flight **(pp. 78-79)** Large. Long black neck. Large white patch beneath chin.

Mallard in flight **(pp. 70-71)** Head noticeable. Short tail.

Cormorant in flight **(pp. 76-77)** Kinked neck. Longish tail.

Cormorant on water **(pp. 76-77)** Thicker neck. White chin. Flatter forehead.

Going further

Further reading

Svensson, Lars and illustrated by Grant, Peter J, *Collins Bird Guide* (Collins, 2004)

Couzens, Dominic, *Identifying Birds by Behaviour* (Collins, 2005)

Sterry, Paul, *Complete British Birds*, (Collins, 2004)

Couzens, Dominic, *Birds: A Complete Guide to all British and European Species*, (Collins, 2005)

Sample, Geoff, *Field Guide Bird Songs and Calls*, (Collins, 2000)

Websites

The Wildlife Trusts

Working together with local communities to protect wildlife in all habitats across the UK, in towns, countryside, wetlands and seas. There are 47 Wildlife Trusts with more than 2,500 nature reserves where you can go to see birds.

www.wildlifetrusts.org

RSPB

Working to secure a healthy environment for birds and wildlife, helping to create a better world for us all. The RSPB has over 150 nature reserves.

www.rspb.org.uk

The Wildfowl and Wetlands Trust

Founded in 1946 by the artist and naturalist Sir Peter Scott (1909 - 1989), WWT has 9 visitor centres around the UK, where people can get closer to birds and enjoy spectacular wetland landscapes.

www.wwt.org.uk

WildSounds

For CDs and videos featuring bird songs and calls.

WildSounds, Cross Street, Salthouse, Norfolk NR25 7XH

www.wildsounds.co.uk

Index